The New Mindful Home

and how to make it yours

Published in 2021 by
Laurence King Publishing
361–373 City Road,
London EC1V 1LR,
United Kingdom
enquiries@laurenceking.com
www.laurenceking.com

A catalogue record for this book is available from
the British Library.

ISBN: 978 1 78627 899 9

Design: Masumi Briozzo
Picture research: Caroline Rowland
Commissioning editor: Zara Larcombe
Senior editor: Gaynor Sermon

Front cover © Saar Manche
Back cover © wij zijn kees

Printed in China

Laurence King Publishing is committed to ethical
and sustainable production. We are proud
participants in The Book Chain Project ®
bookchainproject.com

The New Mindful Home

and how to make it yours

Joanna Thornhill

Laurence King Publishing

Contents

Introduction

Most of us are familiar with the term mindful, or at least have an idea of what it means. The organisation Mindful.org describes it as 'the basic human ability to be fully present, aware of where we are and what we're doing, and not overly reactive or overwhelmed by what's going on around us'. Typically, we think of practising mindfulness solely in relation to meditation – which by its very nature requires us to enter a mindful state – but in fact mindfulness can take many forms, all of which are available to us at any time and require nothing more than practice and awareness. In essence, embracing mindfulness means training our brains to recognise when we are stressed, afraid or overwhelmed, switching our focus away from these thoughts and concentrating instead on our senses (such as our breath, a particular noise or the physical sensations in our body) to knock us out of 'fight or flight' mode.

Statistics indicate that people are spending more time at home now than in previous decades, so it makes sense to consider the role our interior spaces play in our mental well-being, and to use our homes to support this as part of the bigger picture. Creating a mindful home is about far more than simply picking out a wallpaper pattern that cheers us up, or doing a bit of decluttering. It's about paying attention throughout the day to what we surround ourselves with, and questioning what is (or isn't) supporting us, as well as looking beyond ourselves and considering the impact our choices might be having on those around us, and on the planet. By getting into the habit of pausing as we go about our busy lives, to consider and contemplate these decisions in the here and now, we can learn to understand ourselves and our needs a little better and hone an environment that nourishes rather than overwhelms us. As well as what we can see, this relates to the air we breathe, the feeling of materials against our skin and the myriad details our brain is subconsciously processing from all this information, which determine – even govern – our moods, feelings and emotions.

This book aims to demystify the links between body, mind and soul to explain how we can harness the power of mindfulness to help our homes become machines to support our well-being as individuals and that of the planet as a whole. It will help you look beyond fads, trends or shopping 'must-haves' influenced by the 'anxiety economy', and instead consider making slow, gentle lifestyle shifts towards a kinder, more considered way to decorate, curate, clean and manage your home. It will help you create a space that is what you need it to be here and now, be that happy, joyful, calm or stimulated. Tuning into this, and taking the time to notice what is and isn't serving us, is the act of mindfulness itself.

Talking about trends might seem out of step with the wholesome, timeless concept of living mindfully (and indeed, mindfulness itself has certainly entered the marketeers' lexicon of late, with the term 'wellness' being used to flog anything from bedlinen to teapots). Yet in the broader lifestyle sense, trends indicate shifts in the public consciousness towards new ways of thinking. A major study by the Happiness Research Institute in 2019 revealed that feeling

happy in our homes counts for 15 per cent of our overall happiness in life – ranking as three times more important than our income – and that for nearly three quarters of us, feeling happy at home means we feel happy in life overall. Interestingly, the results also show that pride accounts for almost half of our home-related happiness, yet paradoxically it's the emotion we are least likely to feel about our abode, indicating that there's more to repainting a wall and updating our cushion collection than fuelling a shopping addiction. Pinterest reports a rise in searches for 'self-care ideas', so we're clearly aware of the effect our home has on our well-being.

My hope with this book is to cut through the fads to offer real, workable solutions to a plethora of home-based problems that I believe a little mindfulness could rectify – while throwing in a few stylish solutions as well. My 15-year career as an interiors stylist and writer, alongside my work as a regular design reporter for the trends forecasting agency WGSN, had left me well versed in how to pull together a cohesive colour scheme, or where to get a great set of coat hooks, but when it came to the underlying question of *why* we might make these choices, and what (if any) well-being benefits they might bring, my knowledge felt lacking. Like many of us, I spent an extended period at home during 2020 and, as I explored the various facets of living mindfully, my thoughts naturally turned to how I could make my home – and the objects in it – support my quest for enhanced wellness.

Now, more than ever, we are simultaneously more connected and more isolated than ever before, as technology turns so many impossibles into everyday realities while leaving us feeling increasingly out of touch with the world beyond our screens and tablets. It seems even more imperative, then, to harness our homes to help redress the balance, ensuring they offer us peace and sanctuary while still connecting us to nature and the world outside (and minimising the damage we cause to our fragile earth). After all, if we feel disconnected and unhappy with our home, it's hard to prevent this from spilling over into other areas of our lives. It is my firm belief that achieving this needn't be the prerequisite of homeowners alone, or involve spending huge sums of money (in fact, in many cases the opposite is true). Buying a scented candle and a sage stick won't change much, but quiet, longer-term shifts in our thinking, shopping and decorating can start to add up.

Our needs change with the seasons, our circumstances and our passing moods, but by knowing how to determine what we need, and what changes to make to support that, we can create a functioning mindful home to weather any storm. Far from frivolous, the act of (literally) getting our house in order can give us a sense of control, help us feel grounded in a fractious world and even go some way towards helping us become better people.

So, what tangible things can we do to create this mindful home? Well, there are 135 pages to follow on that, but to give you an overview, here are some of the topics we'll cover in detail:

• Creating a friendlier home environment by bringing in softer shapes and silhouettes; nature doesn't do right angles, so seek out rounded corners and cosy nooks for maximum comfort
• How to bring the outside in, be it with plants on a windowsill or using natural materials in furniture, flooring and accessories – and why it can benefit our well-being
• Learn to spot harmful toxins we might inadvertently bring into our homes, and minimise the damage they can cause to our health and the environment
• Creating a dedicated area to practise mindfulness activities, portable or otherwise, regardless of our home's set-up
• How to conduct a mindful audit of your interior, along with ways to declutter meaningfully (and keep on top of it)
• Ideas for introducing crafting, doodling or making into your day, regardless of whether you identify as 'creative' or not
• How to fill your home mindfully with objects that resonate with you and hold (or will allow you to form) happy memories

Go forth and decorate – mindfully.

Mindfulness: the science bit

Research has shown that the brain isn't hardwired, and that we can encourage its neuroplasticity (the ability to create new patterns of thought – aka neural pathways – and override unhelpful default thought processes) to train it to think differently. By doing so, we essentially give our prefrontal cortex (which processes 'executive' functions such as problem-solving and decision-making) a workout, increasing our ability to make rational decisions, helping us to manage our moods and even improving our creativity. In order to forge these new neural pathways, you simply need to exercise your mind regularly and repeatedly through – you guessed it – mindful practices such as breathing exercises or meditation.

CHAPTER 1

Creating a Sanctuary

We often refer to the concept of home as a 'refuge', without necessarily considering what that means to us personally or how we could create this feeling in our own space, particularly if our living circumstances fall short of our own ideal. It can be easy to underestimate the impact of stressors in the home (both in its fabric and in the things it holds) on our well-being as merely aesthetic grievances, but science is now proving that it runs a lot deeper than that.

The Academy of Neuroscience for Architecture has dedicated whole studies to 'neuroaesthetics' (how mood and emotion can alter when we are presented with an artistic stimulus we are attracted to, be it a piece of music or an object of home decor). These have shown that our conscious thoughts aren't always attuned to our environment in the same way as our body is engaging with it, flagging the importance of listening to our design intuition to enable us to create a space where our physiology feels most peaceful – a place where you can come and just be. If you can create that feeling of escape at home, you might find it positively alters how you feel about the outside world, too.

Living with intention

The phrase 'living with intention' can seem elusive and vague. In essence it refers to the way we would like to feel, and the steps we intend to take to achieve that ('I want to feel calm when I meet my friends, so I'll make sure I leave the house with ten minutes to spare so I'm not rushing'; 'I want to feel healthy, so I'm going to cut out sugary, processed foods'). The principles are just as relevant to our homes, too.

On a primal level, it's imperative to our well-being that we feel safe, especially since we have little control over the world beyond our front door. Having rooms and areas that function in different ways - such as a calm bedroom or feelings of energy and connectivity in the kitchen - can enhance this. It's a good idea to begin by taking a step back to assess your space objectively as a whole. Can you identify areas that are causing negative emotions, and what impact that has? Is a cluttered hallway table making it hard to find post and keys, leading you to associate leaving the house with frustration? Or is that pile of paperwork in the living room making it hard for you to feel relaxed in the evening? By working out what these grievances are and how you would like to feel in that space instead, you can come up with constructive solutions.

Once you've set that intention (and taken practical action), take the time to remind yourself regularly of your goals and the steps that will make sure you stick to them. For example, you might have made the effort to clear that messy hallway console, invested in a letter rack to house unread post and hung dedicated hooks for your keys, but the system will need regular maintenance to ensure it doesn't deteriorate when life gets in the way. Rather than berating yourself if or when it does, remind yourself *why* you've set that intention ('I know I struggle with social anxiety, so by ensuring the act of leaving the house is as stress-free as possible, I'm setting myself up to be more likely to enjoy the experience'). Future you will really appreciate it.

See also page 52: Accessorise meaningfully

Living intentionally needn't mean living minimally, although rooms without clutter on the floor and a feeling of uniformity, such as a similar tonal palette without much variation in hues, are less likely to over-stimulate us or stress us out. Conversely, mixing in different textures helps avoid a sterile feel, which could feel oppressive.

The importance of slow living

Modern life certainly has its benefits, yet the number of people suffering from chronic or unhealthy stress and burnout continues to increase. Slow living offers an antidote to this increasing stress by encouraging us to simplify and, yes, slow down our lives. The World Institute of Slowness defines the movement as being about 'time for silence, time for planning, time for observing, time for reflection', and believes that by slowing down, we strengthen our productivity, effectiveness and happiness. Sharing many of the sensibilities of mindfulness, the movement encourages us to concentrate on the present, rather than constantly striving for (or worrying about) what the future holds.

In interiors terms, there are many ways we can embrace the slow-living sensibility. Often, we are so focused on developing or buying time-saving hacks that we inadvertently fail to take pleasure from simple pursuits, such as enjoying the process of calmly making up the bed every morning and using the moment to think about what we want to achieve during the day. In the kitchen, instead of viewing chopping vegetables as a chore and racing to the end, why not invest in a chopping board made from some beautiful wood, stick on a podcast and sink into the process?

Even taking a few moments to really *look* at the objects in your home can bring calm and contentment. You might sit in the same armchair every day, but by dropping your focus on to it and thinking about the day you brought it home, how it made you feel and any happy memories you associate it with can bring that all-important sense of calm. The same goes for anything you've worked on yourself to improve the space: that wall you painted, when you decided at the last minute to mix a couple of paints together to create your own unique colour; the shelf you fixed up that's a tiny bit wonky, but still makes you proud because it was your first time drilling into a wall. If we fail to take the time to notice these things every now and then, it's impossible to truly appreciate them.

Above: If a simple, neutral space feels the most supportive for you, filling it with treasures found on walks, such as dried flowers, will bring both visual softness and memories, as well as connecting you to nature.

Below: We have a tendency, thanks to our primitive caveman-brain, to busy ourselves as much as possible (whether physically or mentally) in order to stay alert and ready to react to danger. Yet this need is often misplaced and simply leads to anxiety. Tending to houseplants is a wonderful way to help us slip into slow living. Take the time to enjoy maintaining and watering them - they will more than repay the favour with what they bring to a space and will give your busy mind an outlet.

Tip

Use your space to aid slow living, particularly during moments of anxiety. Sitting calmly, take a few deep breaths in and out, then shift your focus to details in the room, making non-judgemental notes as you go. Tune out the bigger picture and simply focus on the details and your senses, from the feeling of the velvet chair against your arm or the texture of the floorboards to the smell of a vase of flowers coming into bloom.

Supportive room layouts

Working out what furniture to put where – or even how to configure the bones of our interior spaces – is often done from a practical rather than an emotional point of view. Practicality is undoubtedly important, but considering how a particular configuration will make us feel is crucial to creating a space that supports us and makes us feel happy.

Consider what is more important to you: a feeling of lightness and airy, open space, or a more defined layout that allows private spots (for both people and possessions) so that everything isn't on show all at once. It needn't be an all-or-nothing, however; the term 'broken plan' (or a hybrid floor space, if you will) has made its way into the design vernacular of late, offering a meet-in-the-middle option whereby partitions or picture windows are used to create a sense of flow and openness while avoiding the big-open-box vibe. It's in our nature to seek safe places to hide should the need arise, and walls and doors literally offer that, so removing them can pump up our fight-or-flight response or even heighten adrenaline as our brain tunes in to the fact that there's stuff going on behind us that we can't quite see.

We needn't return to the warrens of tiny rooms typical of untouched period homes, however. There are myriad ways that furniture placement and room layouts – even in open-plan spaces – can provide this sense of security. Try placing key objects, such as sofas and beds, with their backs to the walls (either directly or with a little space in between), and situating dining tables in a corner where possible, to minimise any nagging what's-behind-you anxiety, or opt for high seat backs or wingback headboards to create a similar cocooning effect. Choosing a four-poster bed, or even an overhead fabric canopy that drapes down towards the bed base, could help re-create that cosy den feel we were all drawn to as children. And avoiding hard, sharp edges on furniture can create better flow and give your subconscious one less thing to worry about.

Above: By partially retaining the original wall between these two knocked-through rooms it was possible to create a cosier, more defined dining space within a larger open area, with the table itself filling up a comfortable proportion of the room. If you're considering knocking through walls, talk to your builder about incorporating a 'downstand' and 'nibs' (the term for these retained sections of ceiling and side walls). Hanging a pendant directly over the dining table offers practical lighting and visually anchors the space.

Below: In an open-plan kitchen and living space, a row of base units breaking the space not only helps to define the different zones, but also offers a 'back' to tables and chairs to avoid the potentially angsty feeling of sitting in the middle of a room. The gently tapering shapes of this warm wooden furniture help to balance out any hard edges in the adjoining kitchen area.

The mindful effects of colour

Although we might have a good idea of the colours we're drawn to personally, most of us don't actively consider the reasoning behind these choices, and it's all too easy to allow our excitement over trends to distort our understanding of which tones we feel genuine connection with. It sounds obvious when it's spelled out, but before making any colour commitments – whether in decor or anything else – take a moment to check in with your emotions and think about how you want those colours to make you *feel*.

Colour psychology is a vastly nuanced subject, and although most of us know the sweeping truisms (blue can make us calm; yellow can make us happy), there are myriad factors at play. The applied colour psychologist Karen Haller explains how light enters our eyes and triggers the release of a chemical transmitter, which essentially causes psychological changes, creating an emotional experience: 'Colour speaks to us in language we understand instinctively – the language of emotions – and it influences our behaviour without our necessarily being aware of it.'

Research shows that the wavelength of different colours affects how we relate to them. Tones with a shorter wavelength – blues, greens and warm neutrals – sit in the middle of the colour spectrum, making them effortless for our brains to process (and, as a species, we're programmed to follow the path of least resistance). Colours with longer wavelengths, such as reds, oranges and yellows, appear closer to us than they actually are, and as such can elicit a stronger reaction, hence their association with more stimulating emotions such as joy and passion – or anger and danger.

Regardless of wavelength, as a rule of thumb, the more intense a tone the more stimulating its effect will be (for example, conversely to stimulating red, pink – essentially a diluted red mixed with white – is known to have a calming effect). By taking into account wavelength, tonal saturation and how much you use of a particular colour, you can make more informed design choices and you will be less likely to end up with a space that doesn't feel 'right'.

See also page 28: How to: create a mood-enhancing colour scheme

Above: The paint brand Dulux is renowned for its colour research. Brave Ground – its Colour of the Year for 2021 – was chosen in the hope that it will help to create a nurturing space within which people can express themselves.

Below left: Baker-Miller Pink – a warm bubblegum tone – was identified in the 1970s at the Washington State Department of Corrections as the most effective tone for calming inmates. More recently, the menswear brand Vollebak launched a 'relaxation hoodie' in this specific hue.

Below right: A global survey in 2017 revealed that this particular teal-like shade is officially the world's most popular colour (and was coined 'Marrs Green' in honour of the survey participant Annie Marrs who selected it). If it looks more blue than green to you, however, fear not: scientists are increasingly convinced that we all process colour slightly differently, so there's no right or wrong answer.

Tip

Do you ever find that pure brilliant white feels unforgiving and cool? That's probably because it's a totally synthetic shade, not replicated in nature, so it can be hard to relate to.

Decorating for calm

The idea of what constitutes a calm design is subjective; a minimalist, all-white space might be the embodiment of Zen for some, yet leave others feeling cold and disconnected and even anxious. Regardless of personal taste, however, a modicum of restraint and continuity in the home will help the overarching feeling of calm. This needn't mean creating something bland, so if clashing patterns are your thing, roll with it – but keep a few basic rules in mind.

For continuity, you don't need to follow the same fully cohesive design scheme everywhere (unless you want to), but retaining a 'red thread' can help the flow. Home in on one thing, such as a colour (used as a starring wraparound tone in one room and picked up more subtly as accents elsewhere), a material (rustic wood in a coffee table in the living room, a bench in the kitchen and the panelling around a bath) or even a predilection for, say, block-print artworks throughout. Keeping this cohesion will make you less likely to introduce anything that jars. For example, metal accents needn't be limited to exactly the same metal throughout the whole home, but filling one room with only soft brass accents and another with all chrome may produce an unsettling effect.

Balance is often key to creating calm, and it's well documented that our brains are naturally drawn to symmetrical and reflexive (mirrored) imagery in all forms – including interiors – because they are easier to process. You could include this literally, by placing two matching consoles either side of a fireplace, or opting for his-and-hers sinks in the bathroom, to make things easier for the brain to take in. Less literally, bring in balance by taking into account all the senses, not just sight, when making shopping or styling decisions; for a truly grounding scheme, scent, touch and sound all have a role to play (taste is not so imperative in interiors, although it can still be considered in the broader sense of which spaces feel yummy and indulgent and which leave a bad aftertaste).

In a partially open-plan space, carrying through materials without being too literal helps the flow and is easy on the eye. The rattan of this ceiling light is picked up in the storage basket on the floor in the next room; carrying the same flooring throughout, yet breaking it with a rug, follows the same principle. Curves and softened corners abound throughout both areas, too – as sharp edges can unwittingly stimulate our primal sense of danger, opting for circular shapes can offer natural stress-busting benefits.

Turn down your home

Visual stimulants in the home can be just as detrimental to relaxation and well-being as ingested stimulants such as caffeine. Both can contribute to an anxious, racing mind and an inability to switch off. Yet while we are generally conscious of our caffeine consumption, we can inadvertently binge on the brain-unsettling visual stuff.

Lighting is a good place to start, since too much blue light (such as that emitted from handheld devices) directly before bed can disrupt sleep. In order to preserve the brain's diurnal (24-hour) cycle and enhance its ability to rest and relax, switch from cool white and blue-based light to warmer (and less intense) red-toned light at least a couple of hours before you start winding down for bed. Incandescent bulbs tend to have a warm, gentle glow and a nostalgic charm, but do opt for retro designs that run on contemporary LED strips in place of carbon filaments, as a more sustainable option.

Dimmable lights are hugely beneficial to a nightly winding-down routine, and the much-improved technology and affordability of 'smart' light bulbs, which can be controlled via smartphones or speakers if you don't have traditional dimmer switches installed, offer a great circadian solution. Just as light is important, so too is darkness. The Japanese writer Jun'ichirō Tanizaki extolled its importance in his seminal essay 'In Praise of Shadows' (1933), stating that 'if light is scarce then light is scarce; we will immerse ourselves in the darkness and there discover its own particular beauty.' Allowing space for shadows and darkness helps to create nuance and balance in the home, avoiding over-stimulation.

Commercial packaging is designed to grab your attention and stimulate your dopamine levels, the brain chemical associated with pleasure, so reducing or disguising brand overload in the home is not only aesthetically more pleasing but could also give your mind a gentler time. Seek out smaller brands and independent products with eco-friendly packaging you love for everyday items that you're likely to leave out all the time (and hang on to their bottles and containers for decanting into in the future, too).

Above: Nothing beats candlelight for a comforting low-level glow, particularly in the evenings when we want to lower our cortisol to aid sleep (bright light can raise these levels and trick the brain into becoming more alert).

Below left: A simple string of fairy lights, fitted with warm white bulbs, offers gentle, ambient illumination during gloomy days as well as at night.

Below right: Containers for decanting everyday household items into needn't match. A collection procured over time, mixing shop-bought storage jars with reused jam jars and canisters, does the job on the cheap and looks charming, too. Or simply remove the labels from existing jars and write the contents back on with a glass-marker pen.

Cultural learnings

The last decade has brought a proliferation of ancient cultural concepts pitched as new interiors trends. Yet if you ignore the sales pitches for scented candles and hot-water bottles, these 'trends', although differing in ethos and style, all hold elements of mindfulness at their core and are worth bearing in mind when considering your own decorating.

There is no literal translation, but *hygge* is a Danish term related to cosiness, comfort, feelings of wellness and contentment. While the media often equate this simplistically to log-cabin interiors and fluffy slippers, *hygge* is perhaps better thought of as the idea of introducing comfort and warmth through materials (wood is a great example, but any other natural material with an interesting patina or texture will do the same job) and creating a tactile 'journey' through your space, where similar soft-furnishing materials and accessories are repeated throughout.

The Swedish word *lagom* – roughly meaning 'just the right amount' – works along similar lines to the adage 'everything in moderation'. In interiors this can be translated into pared-back schemes in which clutter is eschewed in favour of fewer, more beautiful pieces that have character and resonance.

The design world has also tuned in to Japan since the mid-2010s. *Kanso* – which relates to simplicity and flow – is one of the seven principles of Zen, and its followers favour modest furnishings and unfussy decoration to aid a calmer way of life. Another ancient yet relevant Japanese concept is that of *ikigai*. Roughly translating as 'a reason for being', it can be found in that sweet spot between doing what you love, what you're good at, what the world needs and what you can be paid for. Although the concept applies to many topics, the writer Tim Tamashiro declares that '*ikigai* leads you to more you and is something to rejoice in.' So creating a home that reflects our own talents and tastes can in turn help us with productivity, and ultimately allow us to appreciate the home even more.

See also page 128: Fashioning harmony in the home

Above: What do you get when you combine Scandi simplicity with Japanese Zen? Yep, you guessed it: *Japandi*. This fusion style typically focuses on honest, beautiful materials and craftsmanship, with black used as an accent.

Below: *Hygge* done right; handled badly, a space like this could simply be wood overload, but thanks to the commonality of the different tones used throughout, and the unfussy matt finish of the various surfaces, this kitchen/dining space is the epitome of kick-your-shoes-off cosy.

Create the perfect space for your personality type

While it's common to consider the set-up of the home in relation to our physical needs, how it can support our mental health is less often discussed. The home is often seen as an extension of your personality – whether self-certified introvert or extrovert – so, rather than concentrating on curating one that simply shows the version of yourself you want the world to see, think about how you can make sure it nurtures you.

Looking at trait psychology is a helpful way to work out our tendencies (and therefore needs) broadly within the home. Personality psychologists often refer to the 'big five' as traits that are present, to a greater or lesser degree, in everyone. These are openness, conscientiousness, extraversion, agreeableness and neuroticism – sometimes referred to as the OCEAN model. For example, if you define yourself as a fairly open-minded person you may be more inclined to make bold decorative choices rather than playing it safe, while those with more conventional leanings may prefer familiar and traditional settings. If you're very conscientious, you're likely to struggle with clutter and will probably flourish best in a home that is super-organised, whereas lower conscientiousness can mean a proclivity towards impulsiveness that might lead to unwise spur-of-the-moment purchases.

Extroverts tend to thrive on company and conversation, so ensuring the furniture is laid out in a sociable way in communal areas, and even opting for larger open-plan, multi-use spaces, will accommodate this. Their need for stimulation could translate into vibrant colours on walls, or energetic abstract patterns on artwork or rugs. Introverts, however, can find that too much socialising leaves them feeling drained, and to allow them the chance to replenish it's imperative that they have a supportive space to retreat to. Introversion is sometimes linked with greater neuroticism, so ensure there are intimate nooks in the home for solitary downtime: a self-contained area for reflective pursuits such as reading and painting could be bliss to an introvert, yet feel painfully isolating to an extrovert.

Above: A bedroom suitable for an introvert needn't be dull. This wraparound wooden 'headboard' creates a cocooning feel to drown out external stimuli, while the built-in shelf and Shaker-style peg rail ensure there's a place for everything. Creating areas devoid of excess ornamentation that contain plenty of negative (empty) space helps guard the mind from feeling over-stimulated.

Below: Plenty of natural light and a plethora of both seating and floor space makes for a happy extrovert. With options for friends or family to perch in the window, relax in a swing seat or sit at the dining table while the host cooks, this informal setting is conducive to chat.

Tip

Unsure of your personality type? Look for online personality quizzes – which are often free – to get to know yourself better. Myers-Briggs, HEXACO and Five-Factor are good places to start.

How to: create a mood-enhancing colour scheme

Articles on colour psychology often explain which colours evoke what mood, but working out how to create a comprehensive decorating colour palette can seem far more mystifying. As discussed on page 18, it's a good idea to begin by identifying how you want a given room to make you feel, rather than how it should look. Here are a few ideas to help you create a bespoke mood-provoking palette.

1. Decorate for rest (blues/greens)
Being harmonious colours (meaning they sit next to each other on the colour wheel), blues and greens arguably encompass the widest variety of tones. Connecting us closely to nature, these hues mix almost magically to create a space that feels balanced and restful. Green brings feelings of harmony while blue helps to pacify the nervous system and can even help to counter sleep disorders.

How to use: Sticking to a strictly tonal palette (where each colour is simply a lighter or darker version of itself) offers the least visual distraction, although it could feel bland; while opting for blue and green hues that are of a similar saturation (such as two light tints or two bold darks) can break things up a little. When your goal is rest, avoid using overly dark or saturated variants of these colours generally, since they can feel depressive – although, conversely, also beware of more vibrant shades of turquoise and lime, which can invigorate.

Pair with: As a 'pure' colour, white brings peace and simplicity, and can appear restful if it is handled correctly (warmer tints will avoid a cold or sterile feel). If you've opted for restful colours in your bedroom but find you need help to get up and go in the morning, bringing in a touch of red can invigorate things, even if it is just as a tiny detail, such as a red mug to drink your first coffee from.

2. Decorate for calm (pinks)

Pinks have quietly overtaken grey in recent years to become a nuanced 'new neutral', and, with the world becoming ever more turbulent, it's arguably not an arbitrary trend. Pink helps to soothe the energy of a room, and can enhance feelings of empathy and love; according to the American Institute of Biological Sciences, it even lowers heart rate and blood pressure.

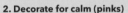 Pink's feminine connotations can make some reluctant to use it in the home (or, at least, not in communal spaces), but less overt tones such as peach, salmon and terracotta are surprisingly easy to live with as a backdrop and bring a warm and welcoming virtual hug to all types of room.

Pair with: For a distinctly grown-up twist, gentle pinks work wonderfully with deeper berry tones and warm rose gold (although in a calming space, keep the berry tones to accents only, to avoid over-stimulation). Green, with its naturally calming properties, sits directly opposite pink on the colour wheel, yet if you choose diluted (rather than vibrant) versions of both tones, the effect will still be harmonious.

3. Decorate for energy (oranges/yellows)

Vibrant, punchy oranges and yellows can lift the soul and boost self-esteem. Prompting optimism and confidence, they're ideal tones for social spaces such as mixed-use, living or dining rooms (orange in particular is said to stimulate the appetite), or even in a children's playroom to evoke fun and frivolity.

How to use: Bear in mind that you can't turn these tones off, so to speak. If you're all-in on the idea of creating a positive, energy-enhancing space, go for broke with these shades – but if the space will also be required for calm and contemplation, you may end up feeling these colours are working against you, causing irritation or even distress. If in doubt, minimise them, or keep their application to transient areas only, such as a hallway or downstairs cloakroom.

Pair with: To (literally) ground their vibrant effects, use tones of brown (including paler shades such as putty and taupe, for a lighter feel). For more contrast, blues can be put to work in several ways: energetic tones such as aqua can help with focus and rejuvenate us, while cooler, seascape tones can temper the scheme and bring balance.

4. Decorate for creativity (purples)

As the colour at the very end of our visible spectrum, purple (encompassing lilac and violet) has long been associated with spirituality and the sense of a higher realm. These long-held ties with reflection mean that it is often associated with meditation, although it's also linked with sparking creativity and curiosity.

How to use: A gentle, misty light to mid tone works well wrapped across all four walls in a study or meditative space, for a subtle lift. Darker purples will bring a punch to a particular zone, such as behind a desk as a feature wall or in a cosy corner on artworks or soft furnishings. Iridescent and pearlescent surfaces on furniture and accessories play with these colours, for an ethereal quality.

Pair with: Yellow complements purple and is also known to aid confidence, so use these two colours if you want your space to fire you up and spark the creative juices. Grey can temper any sugariness in your chosen purple and create a space where external stimulus is dulled, allowing you to concentrate undistracted.

CHAPTER 2

Considered Living

It stands to reason that if we are to create a mindful home, we must be mindful of the cost of what we place in it - financially, yes, but also environmentally, ethically, sustainably and consciously. If we overlook all of these elements and simply purchase on a whim or when we're on autopilot, we do both ourselves and the planet a disservice, and no one wants that weighing on their conscience.

Learning what to look for in order to be more responsible can seem daunting, but it's as much about a shift in mindset as it is swotting up on recycling policies and sustainability initiatives. There are many facets of considered living, from questioning the brands and manufacturers we're buying from, to re-examining the very fibres of our homes themselves, as well as taking into account what we can ethically and responsibly do with our possessions when they are no longer required.

As anyone who's ever watched NBC's *The Good Place* will know, being 'perfect' is pretty much impossible. However, just bringing some mindful awareness to things you'd otherwise buy automatically, and thinking about whether there's anything you could do differently for the greater good (regardless of whether the answer is yes or no), is a great way to start.

Responsible consumerism

Online shopping has made life easier in many ways, but convenience has come at the cost of patience and brought with it a rise of 'instant gratification' culture (and subsequently choice paralysis), as we are presented with a bewildering number of options and are further removed than ever from the producers of our purchases.

Technology itself isn't at fault, of course, and conversely we can also harness it in ways that will help to redress this balance. Keeping lists on your phone of all the things you'd ultimately like to procure for your home (along with measurements of the space you have) ensures that any purchases you make aren't impulsive and wasteful. Or you could create saved searches on sites such as eBay, or stalk your local Facebook 'sell or swap' group, then wait for a match. Technology also allows us to find individual designers, makers and ethical retailers and connect with them on a personal level via their social media platforms to discover directly how they produce or source their wares.

There is often a trade-off to consider. For example, if a cushion is handmade ethically, with an unbleached organic cotton case and an organic wool insert, but shipped from the other side of the world to your home, do the benefits still add up? Think about the 'circular economy' as much as you can, and look for items that can be reused, repaired or recycled when you no longer require them, made with raw materials that can eventually re-enter the manufacturing process, minimising waste.

Looking at the 'value' of something in terms of the care, skill and effort put into its production, and what purchasing it could bring to your life, should be as valid as its monetary cost – and if that means buying less, then so be it. A worthy approach needn't be dull, however: if you're planning a party, for example, instead of single-use plastic balloons and sequin table scatters, choosing homemade tissue-paper pompoms, then using the offcuts and a hole punch to create your own table sprinkles, will be just as colourful and a lot more personal.

See also page 102: The well-being benefits of embracing handmade

Above: Shopping small needn't be daunting. Creative online and bricks-and-mortar businesses – such as Holly & Co's 'work/shop' (a cafe, shop and workspace all under one roof) – are dedicated to shining a light on the incredible power of small businesses. Also look to your local community for initiatives or organisations who are championing the work of local makers and perhaps even offering community, connection and business support as well as a shopping opportunity.

Below: Look further than aesthetics when considering your purchases and educate yourself on who exactly has made that chair or plate you're eyeing up. While many brands may claim to be ethical, some go the extra mile, partnering with charities or social enterprises to produce their wares – such as lifestyle brand Aerende.com (meaning 'care' in Old English), shown here. Consider the issues that matter to you and work outwards from there, be it charities providing opportunities for those with learning disabilities or mental health problems, or simply opting to shop via businesses that champion the work of female makers, or members of the BAME community.

Tip

Help make your shopping habit pay back by signing up to micro-donation initiatives like AmazonSmile, which donates 0.5% of the purchase price of eligible items to a charity of your choice. Or download the altruisto.com browser extension and use this when shopping online: partnered with hundreds of retailers, your shopping will create an affiliate commission for designated charities with every purchase made.

Conduct your own 'greenover'

The term 'greenover' has recently come into parlance, offering a neat soundbite to encourage us to consider what changes can be made – both in design and in efficiency – to ensure that our space is doing its bit for the environment. We all know that bringing down our energy bills is beneficial both to the environment and to our wallets, so to minimise draughts, take the time to add draught-excluder tape around poorly fitting doors and window frames, plug gaps in walls and between floorboards (for the latter, a simple mix of sawdust and flexible wood glue such as PVA does the job brilliantly), and, if you've not got double glazing, fix up secondary glazing film (for the cooler months, at least). Thermal lining for windows can work wonders cutting out chills and reducing external noise, and if you're not a fan of heavy curtains, it can just as easily be added as an interlining in contemporary blinds, too. Conversely, in hotter countries, opting for semi-sheer shades or reflective film on windows (especially in east- or west-facing rooms) can help to minimise heat disruption.

Increasingly, pressure is (rightly) being put on appliance manufacturers to ensure that their goods aren't created with 'planned obsolescence' (where something is made with a deliberately short lifespan, and is hard or impossible to repair when it does break), so if you're planning new purchases rather than procuring second-hand goods, take this into account when doing your research. Consider 'smart' appliances, which intelligently adjust energy usage as required, saving energy over their lifetime.

The last few years have brought a rise in the popularity of open fires and wood-burning stoves, particularly in urban areas, where they are often used in conjunction with central-heating systems. In countries such as the United Kingdom, air pollution is still a top environmental risk to human health, so if you do use fires for supplementary heating, it's important to understand the properties of what you're burning, opting for appropriate fuel and veering towards occasional rather than daily use where possible.

Above: Increasingly, new kitchen appliances are being developed with intuitive features, which save both time and energy – even if the styling is otherwise traditional, like this striking space. Look out for clever features, such as 'smart connected' cooker hoods and hobs that can communicate and auto-adjust air extraction rates when in use.

Below left: Modern wood-burning stoves offer a comparatively more efficient way to heat a space than older models or open hearths, yet choosing the correct fuel is key to capturing these benefits. Whatever your fire type, opt for fuel with a low moisture content (under 20 per cent), such as kiln-dried or seasoned wood, or manufactured alternatives such as fire bricks (compressed and kiln-dried wood particles) or (where appropriate) low-sulphur manufactured solid fuel such as smokeless coal. Kiln-dried products require more energy to produce, but burn more cleanly.

Below right: More is usually more when it comes to curtains, both in terms of looks (designs that only just skim the window can look mean) and insulation. Floor-to-ceiling curtains help minimise drafts and can help visually soften your space. To ensure they don't cut out any light when open, ensure your pole or track is at least 20 cm (8 in.) wider than your window frame (even more, if your curtains are particularly generous).

The beauty of bare surfaces

Regardless of your style or taste, respecting the 'bare bones' of the property you live in, and finding ways to honour them, can bring a grounding sense of calm. This is most apparent in period properties, and a sense of connection to the past and being surrounded by honest, natural materials can – according to the British organisations the Landmark Trust and Historic England – offer the same beneficial effects to blood pressure as partaking in a social sporting activity. Even if your home is fairly new, or has been crudely stripped of any original character, there are ways of bringing the charm back and reaping the mental benefits.

Plaster walls are a case in point. Stripping back layers of wallpaper may reveal the charming original patina of lime or clay plaster, although a modern gypsum-plastered wall can hold a somewhat crisper appeal. Leaving bare bricks exposed can also bring through character, and if the bricks themselves are lacking in charm, painting them could make them work in your scheme, retaining their cosy texture but losing their natural tone. Although bare natural surfaces may still need some finishing, such as a clear protective coating or repointing, leaving such surfaces as they are rather than covering them with additional materials such as plasterboard is ultimately less wasteful.

Wood is a ubiquitous material in our homes, whether in construction – such as floorboards and beams – or furniture. It has long been said to bring a feeling of calm, and a recent psychophysiology study by the research and development organisation FPInnovations revealed that its use in interiors reduces stress and even lowers the heart rate. If your home doesn't contain much in the way of wood, consider bringing in characterful woods through vintage or reclaimed wood furniture and accessories; this has the extra benefit of keeping them out of landfill.

We often form close emotional attachments to our homes and the things in them. If those objects contain elements of honest, perfectly imperfect materials, with a history of their own, this connection can be deepened and enhanced.

See also page 86: Bringing nature indoors

Above: Original period details such as wooden beams are undeniably a desirable feature, creating character as well as offering a link back to the craftsman who originally constructed them. Here, keeping surrounding surfaces crisp and minimal allows them to be the star of the show, while the rustic wooden dining table visually mirrors their colour and patina.

Below left: Original brickwork, if in sound condition (and sealed appropriately), can bring industrial chic to residential spaces, and makes for a surprisingly resilient backdrop in hardworking areas like the kitchen.

Below right: The part-painted wall is slowly replacing the ubiquitous solo feature wall within interiors circles. It can be particularly useful in instances where a contrast is required, such as here: while a completely unpainted plaster wall can appear simply unfinished, by painting two-thirds around the room instead, the look is cool and considered.

Cruelty-free decorating

From fashion to homewares, there has been a seismic cultural shift over the past decade towards both veganism and ethical, cruelty-free animal-derived products. Google searches for 'veganism' alone rose by 600 per cent from 2010 to 2020, and, despite anyone's individual food stance, concern for animal welfare and a desire to do less harm – and salve our collective conscience – is influencing our shopping habits.

Animal products can still crop up in a host of unexpected places, such as candles (some contain stearic acid, which is derived from animal fat) and photographic prints (when techniques such as silver gelatine printing are used). While opting for vegan homewares can sometimes mean compromising other eco credentials (because of their reliance on synthetic alternatives), increasingly, ethically minded brands are using innovative materials and manufacturing techniques, from recycled plastic bottles in place of wool in upholstery fabrics to 'leather' made from apple cores and skins that would otherwise be discarded by the food industry.

That isn't to say that using animal products in interiors is inherently bad. Ethical sheepskin throws, for example, come from high-quality farms, thereby supporting a farming community where animals are well cared for and free to roam during daylight hours. They are a by-product of the meat industry rather than farmed specifically for that purpose, so material that might otherwise be wasted is put to good use. Silk, too, can be more ethical if you look out for varieties such as Ahimsa, which is produced non-violently from hatched silkworm pods, rather than traditionally cultivated silk, which involves killing the moth pupa before it hatches.

On the more purely ornamental side, items such as antlers that have been naturally shed by wild deer can bring warmth and texture into the home, whether displayed traditionally on walls or used in a less obvious way, such as for a table centrepiece. Try local forestry or countryside stores in spring for ready-foraged versions, or pick up your own on a country walk.

Ethically produced natural wool pelts are by nature hardwearing and long-lived and, as a bonus, their unique natural variations are often more beautiful than those of mass-farmed, bleached varieties. If you prefer to shop vegan, look for eco-friendly faux-fur alternatives made from hemp or recycled plastic.

Tip

Interested in less literal vegan-friendly, animal-themed decorating ideas? Look on artist-led sites like Etsy for 3D entomology-inspired wall art, inspired by insects and butterflies yet made from papercuts or papier-mâché. A Google search for 'faux taxidermy' can also offer a wealth of shoppable items or DIY ideas.

Conscientious construction

Whether it's building a dream forever home from scratch or simply adding a modest side-return extension or reconfiguring internal walls, many homeowners will find themselves doing building work at some point. Bringing mindful thought to both the layout and the construction can be beneficial for the environment and your own peace of mind, particularly when the choices you make will influence the air quality of your home.

By designing a space that makes the most of its plot, taking into account how the sun moves around it and how you wish to use different areas, you can minimise the artificial light and heat you need to use during daylight hours, as well as support your circadian rhythms. It makes more sense, for example, to have a large kitchen/dining area flooded with warming, natural light, then exploit any smaller, darker rooms or spaces to create a TV room or den, where low lighting is preferable. If standard windows aren't bringing through enough light, consider 'borrowing' light in key spots via internal glazing, skylights, clerestory windows (rows of glazing above eye height) or even sun pipes, which channel daylight from other areas. In new homes or extensions, installing smart electrical systems from the outset will enable you to optimise and minimise your energy usage, using methods such as geo-sensing or motion-detecting sensors to help you adjust your heating and lighting needs and allowing you to make changes remotely.

When it comes to the building itself, concrete can seem unavoidable in new structures and extensions, but it's worth discussing alternative products with your builders, such as hempcrete (also known as hemplime), which is climate positive (meaning it actively helps remove carbon dioxide from the atmosphere) and purports to have a slew of other ecological and construction benefits. Insulation is imperative for keeping buildings warm in winter and cool in summer, and there are alternatives to the popular polyurethane spray foam and EPS (expanded polystyrene) beads, such as cellulose insulation, made from recycled newsprint, and sheep's wool.

Above: Loft extensions offer the opportunity to play with layouts, in order to borrow light where needed. Here, by opting for a false wall to partially screen a bathroom space, rather than creating two separate rooms, the bedroom is still able to enjoy borrowed ambient light from the window beyond.

Below: Newbuilds or extensions offer the opportunity to think cleverly about visible construction materials. Opting for sheet timber over traditional plasterboard makes it easy to conceal storage in plain sight, by simply constructing it from the same materials as these partitioning walls. Seek kinder materials such as plywood over MDF (both are engineered wood, yet MDF contains harmful VOCs – volatile organic compounds) or cork (discussed on the following page).

41

Friendly materials

Decorating your home with 'kind' materials, be they organic or conscientiously manufactured using innovative resources, is wise. Environmental psychology – which investigates how our well-being is connected to the natural world – has shown that we adapt better to natural settings and materials than to artificial ones, so in our homes the former can feel more relatable than anything synthetic.

Cork, for example, has recently lost its dated reputation as a new generation learns to appreciate its plentiful eco credentials and versatility along with the physical warmth it can bring to the home. It's increasingly cropping up in flooring or moulded furnishings, with designers allowing its natural matt good looks to shine through rather than coating it in the treacle-like synthetic lacquer of its 60s and 70s heyday. In a similarly retro-revival vein, materials such as rattan and wicker are appearing more frequently in interior furniture and accessories thanks to their abundant eco credentials.

Natural cotton and linen are often the fabrics of choice in eco-conscious interiors, cropping up in soft furnishings and even as textural wallpapers. It's worth hunting out organic cotton where possible; it uses far fewer chemical pollutants and less water to produce, although conventional cotton is still a much better environmental option than synthetic fibres, which can release greenhouse gases during their production and shed microfibres into waterways when washed. Hemp and bamboo fabrics are starting to give organic cotton a run for its money. Traditionally used for industrial purposes, they produce strong natural fibres and come from high-yield crops that are sustainable and renewable – look out for them in items such as bedlinen and rugs.

There is also a case to be made for fabrics created from recycled plastics. Although not in themselves natural materials, they qualify for eco-friendly status because they divert materials from landfill or incineration. The more designers and brands experiment with creating commercially viable products from waste materials, the less 'normal' it will become to discard rather than reinvent when a product reaches the end of its life.

The Journal of Consumer Research states that when we are in a negative emotional state, we are increasingly sensitive to (and appreciative of) tactility, meaning that combining natural textures and playing with different materials can be a great way to decorate to support our emotional health. Here, the pleasingly organic shapes of the rattan chairs, combined with a wooden coffee table and textiles-laden linen sofa, helps aid this supportive air.

Setting up a recycling zone

We all know the importance of recycling our waste at home, but sometimes all those separate bins and containers can cause storage and aesthetic headaches. So for the sake of both design appeal and planetary well-being, set up a system that works for you and helps you feel good about what you're doing, rather than gets you flustered over what goes where.

You can buy various freestanding and drawer-insert bins that are specially designed to help with separating recycling, but you needn't be restricted to ugly plastic boxes. Woven seagrass baskets feel far more homely: try placing a few side by side in a corner or under a console table – for ease, you could use a mix of open and lidded baskets, depending on what you're storing. If family members get confused over what goes where, stick a 'crib sheet' inside a kitchen cupboard door, or simply tie a luggage tag to each box or bag stating what goes in it.

Consider setting up smaller storage containers for 'take-back' items, such as used batteries, single-use carrier bags, LED lightbulbs and plastic film. Such products generally aren't included in household recycling but can be returned elsewhere, such as larger supermarkets or your local household waste and recycling centre.

Food waste should be a firm fixture in your recycling area, too; yes, it will eventually decompose with non-recyclable rubbish, but when placed into normal landfill, the lack of oxygen causes it to release methane, which is far more potent than carbon dioxide. In an ideal world, we'd all have the outdoor space and time to cultivate our own compost bins; if that's not an option yet but your local authority will collect food waste, or your municipality has a communal compost area, shop around for a compact metal caddy that looks good enough to keep in full view on a countertop, and add a sprinkling of bicarbonate of soda and a few drops of essential oil to the bottom to minimise nasty whiffs. If you don't have the space even for that, consider keeping a bag in the freezer and adding waste to it as you go; when it's full, simply transfer it to an outdoor food-waste bin or compost heap.

Above left: Freestanding shelving can offer an affordable way to sneak more storage space into a kitchen or pantry/storage area. Smaller, open storage containers - like those on the bottom shelves here - provide a handy spot for storing infrequently consumed items that might require sending or donating to different specialist recycling facilities, such as printer cartridges, electronic gadgets and worn-out crayons or stationery.

Above right: Think outside the box when it comes to storage containers: could some old suitcases, an ottoman or a console table with space for baskets underneath offer a practical spot for bulkier recycling? A space such as this could also be used for collating charity shop donations - once they are full, simply drop the contents to your local donation point.

Below: The natural aroma of woven seagrass storage baskets can bring a subtly pleasant smell to the air - always welcome in hard-working kitchen or laundry spaces. They also offer visual softness to otherwise hard-edged areas with rows of cupboards. An open basket like this offers a handy spot for chucking everyday clean recyclables into, such as paper and card, without compromising on looks.

How to: make your own natural dyes

Are you after an unusual, eco-friendly way to update your soft furnishings or wooden furniture? Natural dyeing ticks all the boxes: easy to do very cheaply, it's a great way to use up kitchen or garden leftovers and create unusual colour with real depth. There are myriad ways of doing it. Once you've tried a few variations you might wish to tweak your method or research specific materials and techniques online, but here is a basic starter guide.

Woods

Choose your materials
There aren't any real no-nos here, just variations to bear in mind. Soft, light woods that are fairly porous, such as pine, will absorb dye more quickly than less pale hardwoods such as oak. Ensure any wood you use is stripped bare, clean and dry before you stain it.

Create your colours
<u>Brown</u>: tea and coffee – make a strong filter coffee or cup of tea (upscale for larger quantities), and let it steep
<u>Red</u>: beetroot – chop and boil for an hour with a two-to-one ratio to water, then puree the mixture in a blender
<u>Yellow</u>: ground turmeric – mix to a thickish paste with a little water
<u>Blue/purple</u>: mash up and strain some dark berries (store-bought or foraged) through a fine sieve, then add a splash of vinegar and stir. Note that this may fade to brown over time

How to dye
1. Since there are many variables, you may wish to test strength and consistency on scrap wood or an inconspicuous area, such as the back of furniture.
2. Rub the dye in to the wood using a lint-free cloth or a paintbrush. Allow to dry, then repeat until you're happy with the depth of colour.
3. Ensure the wood is thoroughly dry, then give it a protective finish with a natural wax, in keeping with the sustainable theme - beeswax, linseed oil or soy wax all work well - before buffing with a lint-free cloth to finish.

Ideas to try

- Dip-dye (submerging only one half of the fabric)
- Ombre (lifting the fabric from the dye in stages, to create a light-to-dark effect)
- Two-tone (dip one end of the fabric in one dye, then the other end with a different dye)
- Tie-dye (to avoid the concentric-rings cliché, which is what many people immediately think of as tie-dye, try wrapping the fabric round a pole bound with string, to create wavy lines)

Tip: Wash your fabric before dyeing, using 2 tsp bicarbonate of soda, baking powder or soda crystals – this will help the dye to take

Fabrics

Choose your materials
Protein-rich fibres take dye most effectively, so look out for wool (pre-made pieces or skeins) and silk. Plant-based fibres such as cotton, linen and flax also work fairly well. Synthetic fabrics are generally not particularly successful, but if you're not wedded to the piece you're thinking of dyeing, it could still be worth a try. Ideally your material will already be a pale tone, to allow the new colour to show clearly.

Create your colours
Experiment with ingredients, but as a starting point here are some popular materials that are commonly used in natural dyeing and that you might already have in your kitchen, and a guide to the colours they'll produce:
Reds: raw beetroot, fresh red autumn leaves, red onion skins
Pinks: avocado (skins and seed), cherries, pickled beetroot
Greens: artichoke, leafy green veg, camomile leaves
Oranges and yellows: turmeric, pomegranate, orange or lemon peel
Blues and purples: purple cabbage, blueberries, purple potatoes
Browns: coffee grounds, loose-leaf tea, walnut shells

How to dye
1. Mix two parts water with one part raw material, chopped (unless it's already small, such as berries), and simmer for at least an hour in a large stainless-steel pan, with the lid on. Strain into a bowl, discarding the raw materials, and return the dyed water to the pan.
2. Meanwhile, prepare the fabric by soaking it in a pan of 16 parts water mixed with one part salt and four parts white vinegar (this will act as a 'mordant' or fixative, helping the dye to adhere). Boil for about an hour, then remove and rinse in cold water.
3. Add the fixed fabric to the pan of dye and ensure it's fully immersed (tongs are useful – and don't forget to wear rubber gloves), before bringing it back to the boil and simmering until you're happy with the colour.
4. Rinse the fabric in cold water until it runs clear, then put it through a cold machine wash before drying naturally, preferably out of direct sunlight.

CHAPTER 3

Mindful Objects

Whether you follow a particular religion, consider yourself an atheist or have your own definition of what spirituality means to you, you're probably familiar with the concept of deities, symbolism and totems. With the increased discussion of mindfulness and its myriad benefits, it's becoming more common in the West to explore elements from other cultural practices such as Buddhism or even Shamanism, adapting them in a non-religious manner to create our own set of symbolic rituals.

Tools and design can help greatly with this goal, and most of us own objects that hold fond memories and help us feel calm and centred, or joyful and grateful, or even remind us of the transience of life. All this can be deeply embedded in our long-term memory, meaning the mere sight of these objects is enough to 'activate' the associated emotions. It is, however, possible to 'train' the brain to make this association with anything, simply by taking a couple of minutes to focus on it every now and again and drink in those feelings, checking in and noticing the physical sensations the object is having on our bodies.

Such objects (and their settings) have the power to change and improve our mood, motivation and energy, helping our home to become a nurturing haven. By incorporating them into key areas of the home, we can enhance harmony and evoke happy memories throughout, in turn lifting our spirits as a whole.

The power of positive affirmations

Although mood and circumstance play a part in how positive our homes feel, there are many ways to tweak things to ensure that we are setting up our space (or, at least, specific areas of it) to aid this as much as possible. One obvious starting point is to spell it out, literally, with some form of positive word-based artwork. The trick is to look for something that holds a personal resonance with you, not merely a generic phrase lifted from a greetings card. It could be something as simple as a print reminding us to 'inhale, exhale' – that may sound simplistic, but using it as a tangible nudge to take even a single deep belly breath when feeling stressed or overwhelmed can offer a useful reset on racing thoughts.

If that doesn't sound like your thing, perhaps a line from a favourite song that always lifts your mood, or a sentence from a favourite book, will suit you better. You needn't be a master calligrapher to create your own; simply type up the quotation in a font you like, then print or hand-copy it on to a sheet of paper or card. A less literal approach could be the strategic placement of a print or artwork with which you have positive associations, whether it's something you inherited from Granny that you always loved seeing in her kitchen as a child, or the work of a local artist depicting a favourite place in your neighbourhood, which makes you think of happy times meeting friends for coffee or walking the dog.

It's all too easy to fail to notice – to really *see* – the pieces we pass many times a day. Habituation means it's in our nature to overlook the familiar once it's no longer novel, such as the buzz one gets from wearing a new outfit for the first time compared to how we feel the fiftieth time we put it on. Training your brain to make, and keep, this image-based association requires a little effort, so try taking a few moments every day to build it up by looking at and thinking about the meaning behind your chosen mood-enhancing piece, rather than letting it become part of the furniture.

See also page 120: Keeping it fresh

Above: Just as curved and rounded edges within design can make us feel subconsciously safer than being surrounded by sharp corners, so too can the so-called 'power of cute', which makes use of simple rounded shapes, as seen in this 'Be Kind' wall print.

Below left: Most design-savvy folk won't want scrappy Post-it notes tacked haphazardly to walls declaring 'don't worry, be happy!' in biro, yet you needn't invest in expensive frames to display said affirmations, either. A casual selection of meaningful postcards, fixed to the wall with a strip of colourful washi tape, or a pinboard fixed to the wall as a makeshift artwork holder, lets you keep a fresh and evolving display.

Below right: The 'inhale exhale' message featured on this pennant flag may be a simple one, but breathing exercises can have powerfully positive effects on our anxiety levels. Use a simple written mantra as a prompt to try a round of helpful techniques, such as 4-7-8 breathing: inhale through the nose for a count of four, hold for seven, then exhale through pursed lips for eight. Repeat for three rounds, to act as a manual off-switch if your fight-or-flight mode is kicking in.

Accessorise meaningfully

Much in the same way as using affirmation-based artwork as a visual prompt, by bringing meaningful objects into key areas of the home (and turning our focus to them), we can train our minds to associate their presence with a particular feeling, such as calm or compassion. This can be achieved regardless of what the item actually is, whether it's a specific ornament added to an altar-like setting or simply a small accessory you engage with every so often throughout the day.

You may wish to choose something with a spiritual aspect (whether you are religious or not), but equally you could choose an item that holds special memories and thus stimulates 'feel-good' hormones, perhaps giving it extra gravitas by placing it under a glass cloche. The idea is that by using the power of intention, repetition and positive thoughts, you can mentally 'charge' the piece so that it reminds you of your intended feeling or emotion. The effect will be easier to achieve if you choose a personal item that already resonates with you, but if you don't have the hand-me-downs or keepsakes to begin with, start your own collection by seeking out locally made artisanal wares or vintage trinkets that feel as though they've got a story to tell, homing in on the objects that seem to truly speak to you.

Physical prompts can be used for specific intention-based interactions, as well as being decorative. Mala beads, for example – traditional meditative tools in Buddhism and Hinduism – are used by setting an intention or statement that resonates with you, then touching each bead in turn and repeating this mantra occasionally throughout the day, to relax you or curb out-of-control thoughts. It needn't be strictly ceremonial; you can apply this approach to the everyday things around you, to ground you every time you use them. For example, when you make your morning cereal, think about the joy you felt when you found the cute retro bowl in the charity shop near your old house, or take a moment to tune in to the sound of the cereal gently filling it, and the way the milk looks as it swirls on top.

Above: 3D objects can work wonderfully as wall art, breaking up an otherwise boxy wall of frames and bringing in an organic, less structured appearance. They can also elevate prized possessions. Consider clever ways to display treasured items, such as these vintage clogs, highlighted by suspending them within an empty frame.

Below: When thoughts are racing, physical objects can be used to ease our minds out of panic mode: as most of our worries are projections about the future or ruminations on what's passed, by shifting our attention to what is right in front of us and objectively noting it, we encourage the brain away from spiralling thoughts and train it onto the facts in front of us. Pick an aspect to focus on as you scan your belongings: observe everything that's red, or mentally note the different textures or materials between objects – whatever helps you bring your attention to the present moment.

Tip

Look out for cultural touchstones, such as these lucky symbols and talismans from around the world:

- **Daruma** 'Lucky God' doll (encouragement and goal setting) – Japan
- **Trolls** (luck) – Scandinavia
- **Dala horse** (strength and dignity) – Sweden
- **Dreamcatcher** (protection from nightmares) – North America
- **Elephant ornaments** (placed facing the front door, to bring good luck into the home) – China
- **Nazar beads** ('evil eye'; protection from harmful intentions) – Turkey

Crystals for mindfulness

Whether you're an all-out believer in their healing powers or dismissive of the mere notion, crystals can be both a beautiful and a useful addition to your home. Different crystals are purported to hold different energies and vibrations, which support a variety of needs or help with struggles we may be facing. In recent years they have become commercialised, but their use as a healing tool dates back thousands of years. Regardless of whether any benefits are down to the stones' inherent qualities or simply the result of the placebo effect, if they work for you, they work.

If you're keen to dabble, start by learning a little about commonly used crystals and their properties. If you're suffering from anxiety, for example, you could opt to keep an amethyst around you (it is said to possess calming properties and aid relaxation), or if you're struggling to focus at work, place an azurite – believed to help with concentration and focus – on your desk.

Committed crystal owners advise 'cleansing' your stones using various methods, such as holding them above the smoke of a burning sage stick, but this could be seen more as simply setting an intention and renewing it with regular cleanses. Say you've opted for rose quartz to help you better express love and gratitude (the stone is said to promote heart healing). By taking the time to hold it and consider your intention regularly, over time you'll train your brain's neural pathways to associate the stone with being more open with your loved ones.

When it comes to the appearance of your home, combining 'plant power' with crystals can bring a double whammy of goodness. This could be as simple as creating a display with an air plant on top of an energising stone, such as selenite, in your main living space (simply fix the plant in place with non-toxic glue), or placing tumbled black obsidian (said to dispel negativity) on top of a plant pot by your front door or in the hall. Incorporating your crystals into an area of your home that you see daily will remind you to connect with them whenever you need a little cosmic pick-me-up.

Above: House-shaped glass terrariums, inspired by Victorian Wardian cases (used originally for housing exotic plants), provide a perfect display opportunity for a prized crystal collection. Seek out crystals that might work together to help support a particular need or desire, or just select what you think looks nice.

Below left: The triangle has many spiritual connotations and is said to symbolise strength, luck and the four elements. As such, it's a shape that often occurs within crystal displays, whether in the guise of a small shelving unit or in glass display pyramids.

Below right: Setting up crystal grids can help maximise the properties crystals hold (as well as creating a pretty styling arrangement). This grid is designed with dreaming in mind, and its choice of stones, including lapis lazuli, jade and malachite, were chosen to help those sleeping here better remember their dreams and encourage their positive influence in waking life.

Hone your vision

Visualisation is the act of focusing on a goal and imagining how it (or you) will look and feel when you get there. A visualisation board in the home can help you define an overarching vision of how you'd like your space to make you feel, or represent other life goals, whether those be long-term ambitions or small, more tangible targets.

The process of creating such a board – and of looking at it regularly – runs deeper than merely visual gratification, however. The neuroscientist Dr Tara Swart explains how these boards 'prime your brain to grasp opportunities that bring you what you want in life … [the] images track instantly to your brain's visual centres, bypassing conscious thought, meaning your brain can't filter them out.'

Before you begin, determine the focus of your board, then consider where it might go, since that will dictate what backing you use. Ideally, it should be placed somewhere you pass often. It needn't be a 'board' at all: a simple sheet of brown Kraft paper could suffice, or a pinboard will allow you to adapt things as your requirements change and you tick things off. If you want to create something a little more permanent, set it up in a frame and hang it on a wall.

Start by gathering anything that speaks to you. Postcards and cuttings from magazines are good places to start, and you can run online searches on sites such as Pinterest, printing out your favourites from the resulting images. Photographs, ephemera, pressed flowers, ticket stubs … look for anything relating to your chosen goal. Cut them out and arrange them in a way that appeals to you, before sticking them down with glue or tape (washi tape always looks nice).

If you're creating your board as an overall decorative guide, feel free to add paint, fabric and wallpaper swatches, too, or even sketch out a rough idea of how your ideal house or space might be. Just don't confine yourself to a particular design aesthetic; the idea is to tune in to the more intuitive, emotion-led side of your brain, rather than knocking up a moodboard for how to redecorate the spare room.

Above: While this process works best when you allow yourself to simply pick images or words you're instinctively drawn to, consider why exactly they are calling to you. Are you drawn to certain images for literal reasons ('I'd love to go on holiday to this beach resort')? Or is it more about what it represents ('this coastline looks so spacious and peaceful and I'd like to feel that way within myself')? Try, too, to seek out images depicting the process for achieving your goals as well as the end result: if you're trying to lose weight, for example, rather than including an image of a 'perfect' model, choose images of healthy meals or people exercising.

Below: When you open your mind and allow it to draw together images and ideas you feel instinctively drawn to, you might surprise yourself when a theme, palette or overall mood seems to naturally emerge. Once it's completed, make the effort to notice and concentrate on your board regularly: your brain will begin 'value tagging', constantly (and consciously) reminding you of what you're looking out for.

Tip

If you'd rather not have something on your walls at all, a sketchbook will also do the job (just keep it somewhere easily accessible, such as in a bedside cabinet, where you can look at it regularly).

Setting up a meditative space

The act of meditating requires no specialist equipment, only an engaged and willing mind, but if you create a designated meditation space at home, your brain's neural pathways will, over time, begin to associate that space positively with the practice. For that reason it's worth trying to carve out a 'sacred spot'.

Firstly, select your area: perhaps a cosy armchair overlooking some greenery, or the floor space at the foot of your bed. You don't need to contort yourself into the lotus position, but it's best to sit upright with your back supported, to ensure you're comfortable yet not likely to doze off. The process should be relaxing, and that may cause your body temperature to drop, so keep a blanket to hand in case you feel chilly. Anything else is really scene setting, although 'props' – when used only during meditation or focused relaxation – can help you to form positive associations, too.

Some practitioners like to bring spiritual significance to their meditative spaces using props that represent the five elements of nature (a plant for earth, for example, or a glass of water for, well, water) or stimulate all the senses, such as sweet-smelling incense sticks or a bell or singing bowl for sound vibrations. Lighting a candle is commonly incorporated into wellness practices, and it is an act that's long been associated with giving thanks or remembrance, in both religious and spiritual settings. All these acts and rituals can become a helpful part of the wider meditation process, and incorporating elements to mark the beginning and end of your practice – such as lighting and blowing out a candle or resetting your space – will help your brain to transition more fluidly into meditation time and return to 'real life' afterwards.

This approach can also be useful if you don't have a fixed meditation space and have to fit ad hoc around other things, people and activities. By associating these portable objects with your practice, simply setting them up anew will signal to your brain that meditation time is coming, and in time, simply looking at them will remind you to be more mindful.

Above: While any comfy surface will do for meditation, if you want to invest in some specific kit, a meditation floor cushion (whether in the style of a cushioned mat or round pouffe) can offer a comfortable way to sit on the floor while supporting joints or elevating hips. And, if you use it only while meditating, it helps your brain shift into meditation mode when you pull it out ready for use.

Below left: Think creatively about where you might carve out a mini wellness space at home. Could a redundant area, such as space under the stairs, be put to the task? By combining yoga bolsters and floor cushions with a cosy armchair and a little foliage, this nook is both cosy and fit for purpose.

Below right: The tops of small cabinets or console tables provide useful surface space for meditative aids such as incense sticks or crystals, allowing you to create a display that looks good enough to leave out permanently. If you are working with a space you need to clear away, keep all your meditation trinkets contained on a tray, allowing you to easily switch uses without having to rearrange everything each time.

Tip

If you're new to meditation, there are plenty of apps that offer free basic access to help you get started. Try Calm, Breethe, 10% Happier, 1 Giant Mind and Headspace to get you going.

The role of rituals

Rituals needn't be 'serious' or ceremonial activities; they can also be integrated into our everyday chores or autopilot activities, transforming tedious tasks into mindful, grounding moments. The predictable repetition of choosing to turn these actions into rituals and doing them regularly will teach your brain what to expect next (often, it's fear of the unknown that can cause cortisol levels to spike), and will in turn reduce stress and anxiety over time.

Certain interiors 'props' can help with this: for example, if you love that feeling of cracking the spine open on a brand new magazine, set yourself up for a short daily read in your favourite spot, put any other distractions down and ensure your favourite beverage or snack is close by. Or, to begin an evening wind-down, use dusk as your daily trigger to focus on mindfully closing the curtains, switching off the main lighting to circadian-supporting dimmer side lamps and maybe lighting a candle, before spending even just a few minutes calmly contemplating the day. Simply taking some deep, restorative breaths in your favourite chair, if repeated daily, should help your brain automatically begin to wind down as soon as you make the decision to go and begin the process.

The same principle can be applied to activities we wish to turn into habit. For example, if you've decided you'd like to take up watercolour painting but are constantly procrastinating about it, anchoring it to a fixed routine – such as after you've put the kids to bed or poured that evening glass of wine – and sticking to it should result in your body naturally gravitating towards the task before your mind has a chance to question it. If a leisurely evening of watercolouring sounds unrealistic in your frazzled life, applying the same principle to something arguably less enjoyable that commonly causes you stress – such as calmly going straight into tidying mode before you sit down for the night, rather than putting it off and being unable to relax in a chaotic room – could also help. Once your brain gets up to speed with your body, the whole thing will require far less effort.

See also page 52: Accessorise meaningfully

Above: Taking the time out each day to diarise your thoughts and feelings can be a really useful way to check in with your emotions and even log any changes in your mood related to your hormonal cycle or external factors. It can be helpful to turn this into something of a ritual, or incorporate it into a routine, such as helping you wind down from work into evening mode, or as part of a pre-bed destressing exercise.

Below: Making up your favourite drink is a great option for turning something otherwise mundane into a ritual: if you appreciate a good cup of coffee, for example, consider curating your own version of a 'tea ceremony' with a grinder, cafetière or pour-over coffee filter, pretty milk jug and your favourite mug, and try taking the time to truly appreciate the making process as much as the consumption.

Sensory ways to lift the spirits

We all need a pick-me-up sometimes, and the multipack of biscuits or trashy TV series certainly has its place. But, rather than always reaching for such habitual comforts, consider turning to more soul-enhancing practices to shift a sluggish mood, using visuals, sounds or actions.

Sound has long been known to influence emotion. A recent study by the Brighton and Sussex Medical School revealed that listening to natural sounds (as opposed to synthetic noises) actually encourages the brain to focus our attention outwards as we tune in, heightening the nervous system's rest-digest activity, which can lower anxiety. Objects that enhance such sounds will therefore bring a grounding relaxation to the home. Wind chimes are a simple example, although if you find the sound of the metal versions irritating, look for wooden, shell, crystal or ceramic chimes for a softer sound to tune in to when the wind and rain pick up.

The sound of a singing bowl, or even a tuning fork moved slowly through your space, will have a similar calming effect. They have long been associated with meditation, and the sounds change as they vibrate (simply tap the tuning fork against a hard surface, or – for bonus points – a crystal). When two different bowls (or forks) that operate on slightly different frequencies are activated together, they can produce 'binaural beats', which are said to improve mood and relax the brain.

Gratitude journals have become increasingly popular in recent years, with practitioners opting to write down three things they are grateful for that happened in the last 24 hours: research suggests that practising gratitude in this way can have long-lasting positive effects on the brain, as well as producing an immediate sense of appreciation. A 'gratitude jar' follows the same principles yet is more interactive, and its mere presence acts as a physical prompt to remind you of all you've got to be happy about. Choose your receptacle, then write down one thing you're grateful for right now on a piece of paper before placing it inside. Aim to use it at least once a day, or even every time you feel gratitude for something.

Above left: Moon phases have long been linked to spirituality and feminine energy – as such, the motif is popular among spiritual practitioners. It also makes for an attractive design motif, such as on these ceramic wind chimes.

Above right: A simple glass jar can work well for storing written gratitude notes – seeing it fill up helps you remember at a glance how much you have to be grateful for. Set aside a special evening when it's getting full to read back over them all before emptying and repeating the process, or dip in when you're feeling down for an instant boost.

Below: Singing bowls originated in ancient China and are traditionally constructed from copper and tin alloy, though in recent years crystal singing bowls have grown in popularity, particularly for 'sound baths' and healing work.

How to: create a mindful totem

Creating your own mindful artwork or totem may help you harness a deeper connection than simply buying something ready-made, and the very process of creating it can be a mindful act in itself. As discussed throughout this chapter, with practice, mentally 'charging' an object with your intention - through focusing on it and holding an awareness of the emotions you'd like it to induce in you - can give the brain an instant visual cue.

The following ideas can be created simply and affordably. Whichever one you choose, programme it with your intention, then display it in a strategic spot, ready to engage with when you need its help.

Ensō circle

A simple yet symbolic brushed circular outline, the Japanese ensō circle is a symbol of Zen Buddhism, referred to in ancient texts as 'a vast space, which does not lack anything, nor does it have too much'. Traditionally the circle is created with one brushstroke and one breath. An incomplete circle represents the beauty of imperfection, while a closed circle symbolises wholeness and the complete circle of life.

You will need:
· Black acrylic ink or watered-down black paint
· Dish for ink or paint
· Paper: any will do, although you may prefer the look of a fine art paper or even stretched canvas if you wish to hang your finished work
· Thick artist's or decorator's paintbrush

1. Pour the ink or paint into the dish, diluting it with water if necessary to obtain a relatively watery consistency, without it being too thin.
2. Lay out the paper, dip the brush in the ink, inhale deeply, and slowly create a circle, moving the brush in one fluid motion from start to finish, ending your stroke as you finish exhaling. The aim is to mindfully finish the shape regardless of how it looks, rather than focusing on the

Artwork by Project Nord

aesthetic qualities. Once you're done, put down the brush and enjoy any imperfections as part of the process.

3. When it is dry, hang your circle somewhere conspicuous to remind you of the open-mindedness and acceptance it represents.

Crystal terrarium

Whether you view crystals as powerful vibration-rising super-totems or simply like their pretty looks, an arrangement in a contained display space such as a glass terrarium, with a few plants for softness, is portable (so that you can bring it directly into a meditation practice) and will help your mind to access the stones' healing associations. You could create one featuring your favourite stones simply arranged on instinct, or curate a collection with purported benefits to a specific area you want to work on, such as easing depression or enhancing relaxation.

<u>You will need</u>:

· Glass terrarium: retailers offer metal-edged faceted designs (pyramid shapes are popular, in part because of the associated spirituality of triangles). A cloche shape will look simpler and more rustic, and an open bowl without sides might be preferable if you want to access your crystals regularly. For a low-cost alternative, repurpose a Kilner jar or even a large jam jar (with its lid, to create a closed terrarium, or unlidded, to turn it into an open vessel)
· Pebbles
· Horticultural charcoal (for closed terrariums)
· Potting medium: houseplant potting soil for closed terrariums, succulent potting compost for open vessels (assuming you're planting succulents, that is), sand, shells or pebbles for air plants
· Plants: for closed terrariums, look for slow-growing, humidity-tolerant varieties that cope with low, indirect light, such as miniature ferns, boxwood or pilea, ensuring they're not planted too close to the edges. For open terrariums, try hardy sempervivum, echeveria or agave
· Crystal(s) of your choice

1. Make sure your vessel is clean and dry, then line the base with pebbles to a depth of about 2 cm (1 in.). If you're making a closed terrarium, add a layer of horticultural charcoal on top of the pebbles, then add the potting medium.

2. Plant up any soil-growing plants, making sure they're not too close to the edge of the container, then add your crystal(s) (and air plants, if using) to the setting.

3. Place your terrarium wherever it will be of most use to you, avoiding direct sunlight; a relaxing arrangement may make most sense on a bedside table, whereas a creativity-enhancing set-up could be a great option for a craft space.

Tip

Crystal combinations and properties:
<u>Ease anxiety and depression</u>: tiger's eye (bravery), obsidian (shields against negativity), amethyst (balances irritability and mood swings)
<u>Spark bright ideas in your workspace</u>: citrine (creativity and self-expression), green aventurine (clears blocked energy), haematite (improves concentration), shungite (said to filter out electromagnetic frequencies if placed between you and your computer)
<u>Encourage calm and sleep</u>: lepidolite (promotes deep relaxation), lapis lazuli (for dreaming), angelite (brings peace to the mind)

CHAPTER 4

Clean Living

For years, we've been sold the idea that bacteria is the enemy, with the media and manufacturers of cleaning products encouraging us to bleach and sterilise our homes in order to stay healthy and happy. But this approach has led to the 'hygiene hypothesis' put forward in the late 1980s by the scientist David Strachan, whose initial research suggested that our sterile modern world has resulted in limited exposure to micro-organisms, resulting in a rise in medical complaints such as asthma and allergies. Latterly this idea has been refined and backed up by Professor Christopher Lowry, whose research has revealed the role of beneficial microbes in our environment, and how without them we are more vulnerable to inflammation and even stress-related psychiatric disorders.

This chapter isn't (just) about 'cleaning' in the literal sense. It's a deep dive into the many ways that creating a less toxic home can improve our physical and mental health, as well as the health of the planet. By taking a more mindful approach to what we bring indoors and reaching for natural scents and cleaners over mainstream big-brand products, we can naturally purify the air in our homes and minimise the harmful effects of chemicals and toxins that we might not even realise are present.

Evoke emotions with essential oils

Scent is processed by the brain in much the same way as memory, retrieving and replaying it when activated, hence its ability to transport our minds elsewhere and even transform our mood. Natural fragrances make us feel connected to nature and can evoke happy memories, such as of playing among freshly cut grass as a child or smelling those comforting Christmas spices often used in cooking during December. Essential oils, so-called because they contain aromatic compounds or 'the essence' of plants and vegetable matter, are an easy way to bring these natural fragrances into the home. They are said to stimulate the limbic system – which is in part responsible for this memory-forming capability, as well as helping to regulate breathing, blood pressure and stress hormones – hence the oils' link with calming and mood-enhancing benefits that synthetic scents simply cannot bring.

Basic oil burners (commonly a ceramic or copper bowl suspended above a tealight) and electric vapour diffusers essentially do the same job. The latter is better for larger spaces or areas that you might leave unattended, while a traditional oil burner is a safer option for areas such as a bathroom, where plug-in devices are not appropriate. Candles appeal to both sight and smell, and the benefits are far greater when they are fragranced with essential oils than with synthetic. Look out for the quality (and quantity) of the oils you use, how they are mixed and what emotions each combination is likely to evoke. A higher concentration of oil offers a stronger scent (and increased cost), making it more potent. Opt for kinder alternatives to paraffin wax, such as soy, which is vegan and obtained from a renewable source, or beeswax, which is a by-product of the honey industry and, thanks to its higher melting point, results in a slower-burning candle.

If candles aren't your thing, incense, in the form of cones, sticks or powder, is a great alternative. It offers a stronger burst of emotion-enhancing fragrance, of particular benefit during warmer months, when a flickering flame might be blown out by a breeze from an open window (or even trick your brain into feeling hotter during a balmy summer's evening).

Above: Designers and makers offer ever-more beautiful handmade holders for incense that feel far removed from the clunky models of yesteryear. If you've been put off by overpowering synthetic scents in the past, try incense made using traditional methods and fragranced with essential oils. The scents are far more nuanced and, although more expensive than mass-produced versions, they will last far longer.

Below left: If funds are limited when it comes to candles but you don't want to sacrifice quality, look out for independent brands offering small-batch, direct-to-consumer or even subscription companies to cut out the middleman and keep costs low.

Below right: There are a vast array of diffusers on the market today, from futuristic-looking light-ups controlled by phone apps to simplistic ceramic designs with a sculptural aesthetic, so whatever interior style you prefer, you should be able to find something to blend in (or stand out).

Tip

Buy good-quality oils for maximum benefit. If in doubt, check the labels – good oils are pure (not cut with vegetable oil) and will have their Latin names and country of origin printed on the bottle. Here are five useful oils to get you started, for adding to your oil burner or vapour diffuser:

Lavender = aids relaxation
Sandalwood = sharpens focus
Peppermint = boosts energy
Bergamot = helps manage stress
Rose geranium = boosts mood and happiness

Simple ways of reducing household toxins

For a happy and healthy home, the purity of the air we breathe is just as important as its scent, yet in today's modern homes, air quality can sometimes be no better than outside. There's even a name for it: Sick Building Syndrome. The area is still under-researched, but it is believed that fumes or fibres emitted from flooring and furnishings, combined with poor ventilation (common in newer buildings), can cause headaches and even breathing difficulties. Evidence seems to point towards volatile organic compounds (VOCs) as key culprits; these are emitted by various finishing materials (such as paint and flooring) as well as furniture and fabrics.

Simply cutting out these toxins is the best approach. Choose benzene-free paint and glue, and look for wooden flooring and furniture that contains no (or low) formaldehyde (whether from the wood itself or the glues and varnishes used in its construction). Some natural materials, such as pure wool, can help to neutralise contaminants in the air: opting for 100% wool rugs is an easy way to bring in this benefit (rugs and hard floors can be better for asthma sufferers than carpet). Plants can also absorb airborne VOCs, and studies have revealed that they store these particles in their leaves and roots.

Every so often, scare stories in the press warn about electromagnetic frequencies (EMFs), referring to non-ionising radiation emitted from household electrical appliances such as microwaves, mobile phones and Wi-Fi routers. But there's debate about whether such EMFs are strong enough to cause health problems. While there's a burgeoning market in home products that claim to combat electromagnetic stress, there are natural alternatives, too. Himalayan salt lamps have been shown to generate small quantities of negative ions, which can increase the flow of oxygen to the brain and bring myriad other wellness benefits, especially when lit (because the warmth generated by the bulb is said to release more ions). It is not clear whether they release enough to bring about these benefits, but they certainly won't do any harm.

See also page 88: The benefits of owning houseplants

Above: If you prefer full carpets to area rugs, opt for a design made from natural materials such as coir or sisal, which will contribute to the air quality of your home (especially if it ends up covering a large surface area). Beware any 'hidden' toxins in carpet backing materials (such as styrene butadiene, which is linked to Sick Building Syndrome) and choose eco-friendly underlay (felt or wool are good options).

Below: Traditional and ancient paint made predominantly from limestone has enjoyed a renaissance in recent years, both for its gentle, textured appearance (resembling tinted fresh plaster) as well as its eco benefits. Bauwerk lime paint, as seen here, is made entirely from clay, minerals and natural pigments, so is naturally VOC-free and completely non-toxic.

Introducing cleansing rituals

A smoke-cleansing ritual involves lighting specific herbs, woods or resins and allowing the smoke to waft through the space while you take a mindful pause to set a personal intention or repeat a mantra, consciously (and figuratively) let go of thoughts that no longer serve you and allow positive intentions to take their place. As its popularity has risen, there has been something of a backlash over the perceived appropriation of this sacred ceremony, which is known among Native American and other indigenous communities as 'smudging'; the term 'smoke cleansing' isn't tied to any religion or community, so is perhaps the most respectful way to refer to the practice. Whether or not you choose to do it for spiritual reasons, the practice can be a useful way to find focus and quieten any 'monkey mind' chatter that might threaten to overwhelm you, as a mindful calming technique.

Alongside its meditative qualities, the practice is rooted in very tangible properties. The smoke from burning white sage can purify and disinfect the air, which can be particularly beneficial to allergy sufferers, while the compounds it releases can activate the areas of the brain responsible for lowering stress and even the perception of physical pain. Other dried herbs (whether 'sacred' or otherwise) that work for cleansing include cedar, sweetgrass, lavender and common garden (rather than white) sage, and each is purported to bring unique well-being benefits.

There are no real rules with cleansing rituals, though one common practice is to light your chosen herb or wood then reflect on what you'd like to bring in and out (such as welcome in compassion and let go of resentment), before slowly moving throughout your space, allowing the smoke to reach all four corners of the room. A fireproof container or plate is useful for storing your herbal supplies, as well as to catch embers during the ritual and to stub your stick out in at the end. Clay vessels or the traditionally used abalone shell are good for both storing and stubbing out burning herbs. While some practitioners like to spread smoke with a fan or feather, a simple waft of the hand will suffice.

Above: Lighting sage over a candle can help create more of a ritual around smoke cleansing practices. As well as performing the ritual on your space, it can also be used to intentionally clear or 'reset' the energy held within certain objects to take them back to neutral, such as second-hand items being introduced to the home, crystals, or tech like mobile phones.

Below left: Buying your herbs from sustainably harvested sources is important - for the sake of any doubt, you could even try growing your own, depending on what's native to your area. Simply harvest your chosen herbs and tie into bundles (separately, or get creative and combine a few different types) using twine, then leave them to dry out for at least two weeks before using.

Below right: Palo santo - meaning 'holy wood' - is considered sacred in its native South America, and believed to work as an energetic cleanser when burned. It's illegal to chop down these trees, yet their popularity in the West means demand is high, so if you want to enjoy its delicate, sweet scent at home, ensure you shop ethically by checking the small print - the seller should declare how they comply with importation regulations.

Smoke-free solutions

In areas where health and safety regulations might prohibit naked flames, or for anyone concerned about carcinogens or toxins in smoke, or with respiratory conditions, smudge sprays and mists offer an alternative to smoke cleansing. Designed to be spritzed into the air in a similarly ritualistic way, they contain essences of the herbs commonly used in smoke cleansing, such as white sage and palo santo, and can be useful if you'd like to indulge in the ritual when a naked flame isn't appropriate.

If you're not convinced about their energetic cleansing properties, think of them more as supercharged portable air purifiers that you can also spray on to clothes and linen, while reaping the benefits of the specific oils. You can buy various ready-made blends, but it's also possible to make your own (see page 81 for recipes).

Japanese hiba oil is becoming increasingly talked about in the West because of its proven natural antibacterial, deodorising and relaxing qualities. It is sold with wood shavings from the tree itself (ethical sellers will use scraps left over from the construction industry, rather than chopping down virgin trees), and combining the two creates products that repel insects, dehumidify the air and even sanitise the bottoms of bins. Seek it out online or in specialist Japanese shops.

Another beautiful and natural way to bring both decoration and clean scents into the home is through the much-maligned potpourri. The cultural shift away from chemical fragrances has stimulated an emerging market for organic luxury potpourri, featuring pretty petals and complex mixtures of essential oils more suited to the high-end perfume market. Left to infuse and percolate for months or even years at a time, it offers a far more intense fragrance than its budget counterparts, and a single bag can be used sparingly to create ambient scent throughout the home. To make it more affordable, keep it in your own containers (any small open dish, or even an empty tealight holder or candle votive) rather than purchasing any 'official' vessels, and choose blends that contain natural moth- or insect-repelling ingredients, such as cedar shavings or dried mugwort, to tick that 'both useful and beautiful' box.

Above: We all know it's what's inside that really counts – but a bit of pretty packaging doesn't go amiss, either. Not all brand labels are designed as tastefully as this one so if you'd like to leave a room spray out on display and it doesn't already have a lovely label (or you're making your own), look on sites like Etsy for DIY printable labels to suit your aesthetic.

Below: If you're up for a spot of DIY, try making your own potpourri. Collect your preferred mix of flower heads (or petals), herbs and spices, add rock salt crystals to absorb and diffuse the scent, and spread everything out to dry completely for at least a fortnight on parchment paper or in a sealed cardboard box. Transfer to a jar, then add a few drops of your favourite essential oils before sealing and storing in a cool, dark cupboard for at least a few weeks (the longer you leave it, the more potent it will be).

Emerging materials

As humans, we are drawn to natural materials over artificial, so it makes sense to incorporate as many as possible in our homes. In recent years, warm-hued metals such as brass and copper have overtaken the somewhat cold and clinical stainless steel, arguably because the range of tones in these alloys – from earthy browns to rusty ambers and turmeric yellows – feel more closely aligned with nature (and related to energy, happiness and optimism). Designers are embracing their natural patina, which works particularly well in lighting and home accessories, using hammered or oxidised metals rather than anything too highly polished for a more authentic, rustic look. The antimicrobial properties of both brass and copper make it a popular choice for kitchens and bathrooms, too.

Stone and clay are also being used in interesting ways in the home, following more rough-and-ready 'naive' designs for a look that feels closely connected to its organic form. Natural stone floors with variegated and textured surfaces create interest, particularly the naturalistic honed or tumbled ones rather than the glossy (and somewhat artificial-looking) polished styles, and those finished with a water-based matt sealant rather than gloss. Seek out vases, ornaments and other objects in organic shapes, or even furniture incorporating clay (or clay-mixed composite), such as an insert in a cupboard door or a ceramic base to a wooden tabletop. Rough textures bring a wonderful contrast to otherwise slick surroundings, and have a magnetic tactility.

Innovative new brands are leading the way by exploring the possibilities for making homewares and even building materials from bioplastics and biomaterials (produced from renewable, biodegradable sources) rather than fossil-based polymers. By experimenting with the properties of unusual sources including sea algae, corn, castor bean oil, sugar cane and even beetle exoskeletons, designers are creating completely new materials that can be used in innovative ways, such as in heat-pressed moulds or even through 3D printing, to create tableware, decoration and furniture.

See also page 42: Friendly materials

Above: Danielle Trofe is among a number of designers experimenting with mycelium, a vegetative body of fungi, which produces mushrooms. By combining its spores with other materials such as wood shavings and straw, it can be literally grown to form solid shapes - like these lampshades - which are sustainable and biodegradable.

Below left: Inspired to do something with tea waste from offices and cafes in their area, design collective Dust London developed a method for combining the dried-out bags with a non-toxic binder to produce vases and plant pots, which are tinted naturally using the leftover tea.

Below right: Rustic wood as an interiors feature is certainly nothing new - but the way we are choosing and treating wood is shifting. As we turn away from heavily lacquered pieces with 'perfect' finishes and embrace raw materials a little more, unfinished pieces proudly showing their scars and splits become favoured over anything too polished.

Cleaning with natural materials

For good physical health, it is essential that we live in a sanitary environment, but many of the commercial products advocated by 'cleanfluencers' are laden with harmful chemicals such as phosphates, bleach and compressed gases, which contribute to global warming and air pollution and can be toxic to marine life. They take their toll on us directly, too, and can cause skin irritation and even breathing difficulties. A study carried out at the University of Bergen in 2018 revealed that regularly using shop-bought cleaning sprays can affect lung health as significantly as smoking 20 cigarettes a day.

Companies are increasingly offering eco-friendly cleaning products and paraphernalia, but some have less reliable credentials than others, so if you can, consider making your own (turn the page for a range of simple recipes). The kit we use to clean with is equally worthy of appraisal. Most single-use sponges, for example, are made from non-recyclable polyurethane foam, which contributes to the production of harmful chemicals and irritants during both its production and its incineration at the end of its life. It also doesn't biodegrade if it goes to landfill rather than being incinerated.

The humble loofah (or *luffa*) is – despite common misconceptions – the fibrous flesh of a gourd that you can grow in the garden from seed (cool climates may need to start them off indoors), then slice into scrubby pads. Being tough yet non-abrasive, the loofah is a great alternative to harmful synthetics, and can be used for several weeks before being discarded in the compost. Various eco-conscious retailers are stocking up on sponges and scrubbers made from equally ethical materials, such as biodegradable wood cellulose, coconut fibres and sisal, along with bamboo sink and toilet brushes with replaceable heads that, as a design bonus, look a lot chicer than the garish plastic alternatives. Though, in the true spirit of sustainability, do use up all your plastic cleaning implements first until they reach their end-life before investing in alternatives.

As well as paying attention to cleaning utensils themselves, be mindful of other potentially wasteful items you might be using regularly, such as paper towels and disposable cleaning wipes. Consider reducing your dependence on them by simply cutting up old fabric (damaged clothing, frayed old towels or sewing scraps) and storing a small pile close to hand in the kitchen – an open basket is ideal. Use them to wipe down surfaces and clean up spills as necessary, then simply chuck them straight in the washing machine. If they're made from natural materials, such as pure cotton, they can even be cut up and added to a compost bin once they're no longer serviceable.

Tip

If you're up for a simple sewing challenge, try making your own 'unsponges'. There are myriad tutorials online, but in essence, cut two small fabric rectangles, sew three sides together, stuff (organic cotton stuffing is a good eco option, or simply cut fabric scraps or polystyrene packaging 'noodles' into small pieces) and sew up the opening. For added abrasion, use terry towelling on one side, or a layer of mesh (try saving some from supermarket vegetable packaging).

How to: create a chemical-free cleaning kit

The internet is awash with ideas for DIY cleaning products, but the advice varies wildly and brings with it the risk of leaving you so overwhelmed that you simply stick to your usual supermarket sprays. This go-to collection will enable you to make effective, environmentally friendly and lush-smelling cleaning products using everyday ingredients that are all safe and harmless (but always do a patch test first if you use them on fabrics or precious pieces).

Store cupboard basics

Aim to buy large containers of these, to save cash as well as minimise packaging. While some aren't exactly supermarket staples, all are easy to find online or in health-food shops and pharmacies.

• **Bicarbonate of soda** (baking soda): use for abrasive, deodorising cleaning products

• **White vinegar** (distilled is generally considered best for cleaning): known to kill various bacteria and viruses as well as deodorising

• **Water**: some DIY cleaning experts advise using filtered water, but you can also use boiled and cooled water, or tap water left in a jug overnight (to give chemicals such as chloramine and fluoride the chance to evaporate)

• **Olive oil**: useful for conditioning natural surfaces such as wood, rattan, stainless steel and cast iron

• **Castile soap**: an invaluable base for cleaning recipes where degreasing and dirt-lifting is required

• **Witch hazel or vodka** (or other colourless spirit): essentially both do the same job of deodorising, degreasing and disinfecting

• **Essential oils**: opt for those with antimicrobial or antibacterial properties (and delicious scents), such as lavender, peppermint, grapefruit, eucalyptus, bergamot, pine and tea tree* (use singly or combine as you wish)

• **Citrus rinds and sprigs of fresh herbs** (such as lavender, thyme or rosemary): an alternative to essential oils when fermented in vinegar, these give off similarly pleasing scents with the added antibacterial properties of the citrus rinds

• **Spray bottles**: for storing your DIY cleaning sprays. Essential oils can permeate and degrade plastic, so glass is best. Amber or blue glass will filter out UV light and preserve your cleaning products for longer

• **Glass jars**: for storing fermenting vinegar and herb/rind mixes as well as dry cleaning ingredients (repurposed glass food jars will do just as well as shop-bought storage jars; just make sure they're spotlessly clean)

Note: It's great to get creative and come up with your own products, but there are a few rules: don't mix castile soap with vinegar (it makes a gunky mess) and – contrary to popular belief – combining bicarbonate of soda with vinegar can cause them to counteract each other, despite the satisfying fizz.

Recipes

HOUSEHOLD CLEANING

All-purpose cleaner**
· One part water
· One part vinegar

Fragrance: if using essential oils, add 10–30 drops of the oil of your choice; if using herbs or citrus rind, add a few sprigs or a handful of rind.

For an essential oil spray, simply combine all the ingredients.
For a citrus or herb spray, combine the vinegar and citrus or herbs, then leave for a couple of weeks to ferment (store in a glass jar or in your spray bottle, leaving enough room to add the water later). For a longer shelf life, strain out the rinds or herbs before use.

<u>Variations</u>
Toilet cleaner: spray into the bowl before sprinkling bicarbonate of soda on top (as it's added later, the bicarbonate of soda acts as an abrasive and doesn't react with the vinegar). Leave for 15 minutes, then scrub and rinse off.

Glass/mirror cleaner
· Water
· Black teabags

Boil an appropriate amount of water for the size of your spray bottle, then put it in a jug with the teabags (the larger the bottle, the more teabags you will need to produce a strong tea). Leave it to infuse for an hour or so before removing the teabags and transferring the water to a spray bottle. The tannins in the tea will help to remove dirt and grease, as well as providing a streak-free shine once buffed.

Scrubby surface cleaner (for trickier stains in kitchens and bathrooms)
· 120g (1 cup) bicarbonate of soda
· about 60ml (1/4 cup) liquid castile soap
· Small jug of water
· Essential oil(s) of your choice (at least 15–20 drops)

Mix the ingredients to create an abrasive paste, altering the amount of castile soap or adding a little water if required. This cleaner is ideally stored in a shallow container, so that you can dip in a cloth and rub it on to surfaces. Rinse well afterwards to avoid residue.

Natural surface cleaner (for marble, granite and other stone)
· 450ml (2 cups) warm water
· 1 tbsp (15ml) castile soap

Simply mix and spray. Vinegar can erode porous materials, so use this recipe instead of the all-purpose cleaner to protect them.

Wood surface cleaner
· 225ml (1 cup) vinegar
· 225ml (1 cup) olive oil
· 15 drops essential oil

Simply mix and spray. For a longer-lasting cleaner, substitute jojoba for the olive oil. This cleaner will also remove smudges from stainless steel.

Drain unblocker
· 100g (1/2 cup) salt (any kind)
· Freshly boiled water

After removing any physical obstructions, pour the salt down the clogged plughole, followed swiftly by a kettle of boiling water. Repeat as required. (Tip: for more severe blockages that require a shop-bought solution, look for eco-friendly enzyme-based drain cleaners rather than toxic chemical versions.)

All-surface floor cleaner
· 225ml (1 cup) white vinegar
· 1 tbsp (15ml) castile soap
· 15–20 drops of essential oil or a handful of citrus rind (if the latter, ferment before use, as before)

Mix all the ingredients in a bottle, then add to a bucket of warm water (experiment with the concentration, starting with roughly a capful per bucket). For very dirty floors, add 1 tbsp (15ml) bicarbonate of soda to the solution, then rinse with plain water to prevent smears.

Scenting and purifying
Carpet and rug deodoriser
· 150g (1 cup) bicarbonate of soda
· Essential oils (20–30 drops) or 1 tsp (5ml) dried herbs or dried citrus peel

Mix the ingredients in a jar and leave overnight, then sprinkle over carpets and rugs and leave for a day before vacuuming (a small sieve will help you sprinkle, or use a salt or flour shaker to store and shake from).

Air freshener spray
· 170ml (3/4 cup) water
· 2 tbsp (30ml) vodka or witch hazel
· 20 drops essential oil(s) of your choice

Mix the ingredients in a spray bottle and shake before each use.

<u>Alternatives</u>
Swap essential oils for lemon rinds (ferment as per the all-purpose cleaner instructions) to use as a sanitising spray on door handles and so on.
Make your own smoke-free smudge spray (see page 74) by using white sage or palo santo as your essential oil; optionally, add a couple of teaspoons of sea salt for its cleansing properties, or a favourite crystal, then focus on spraying the corners of the room.
Make a calming mist for use during times of stress or to aid sleep and relaxation by choosing essential oils such as lavender, camomile, bergamot and geranium (use as many as you like) and spraying into the air or on to your pillow before bed.
Spray the air-freshener spray on clothes to freshen them between washes, or just before ironing for a blast of heat-activated scent.

---

* Tea tree oil can be toxic to pets if ingested, so avoid it or use with caution if you have furry friends at home.
** It's advisable to avoid using vinegar and bicarbonate of soda on certain natural surfaces, such as granite, marble and stone. Try making the natural surface cleaner for use here, instead.

CHAPTER 5

Becoming Biophilic

The term biophilia – coined in 1984 by the biologist Dr Edward O. Wilson – refers to 'the innate sense of belonging to the natural world'. Wilson noted that humans are 'inherently attracted to the living and life-like forms often encountered in natural environments'. Yet with 60 per cent of the world's population expected to live in urban areas by 2030, it stands to reason that we are increasingly experiencing a sense of disconnect as we distance ourselves from rural or agricultural existences and surround ourselves instead with artificial and manufactured environments. Our mental health can suffer as a result.

The idea of biophilic design is often simplified in magazine articles as something to be achieved by simply buying another succulent or choosing a foliage-patterned cushion. That's not to say that such small touches don't help, but biophilia runs much deeper. At a fundamental level, using design to bring the feeling of the outdoors into the home can help to satiate our primal yearnings, allowing us to see, smell and touch nature when we're in an environment that would not traditionally be conducive to it. By exploiting the various ways we can use our design choices to rebuild this natural connection – through decor, colour and furniture, and by reintroducing natural materials – we can create a happier, healthier home that supports the entire household.

The importance of biophilia

Simply being in the presence of nature brings proven benefits, and the Japanese practice of forest bathing (*shinrin-yoku*), recently popularised in the West, exemplifies biophilia. It has been maligned in the press as a gimmick, but a study at the Nippon Medical School in Tokyo showed that NK cells in humans – those responsible for the function of the immune system – were more active for at least a month after a weekend spent immersed in the forest, possibly aided by the prevalence of the compound phytoncide emitted by plants and trees, which is found to decrease cortisol. Bringing this principle into the home by incorporating wood as a material for walls, floors and furnishings has been shown to decrease stress: an Austrian study revealed that by drastically increasing the amount of real wood in a comparative classroom setting, over a year, the pupils' pulse rates lowered while test results and attendance improved.

We tend to think of natural colours as calming blues and tranquil greens, but nature's palette runs a wide gamut. There are various online quizzes that will help you to determine your 'seasonal' personality, but when it comes to decorating, it can be helpful to consider which tones you're naturally drawn to. Do you love the fresh, pale, powdery tones of spring or prefer the rich, warm, comforting hues of autumn? Does the relative starkness of winter leave you feeling down, or do the contrast and striking silhouettes of a bare landscape invigorate you? Bearing these thoughts in mind – and also considering how these preferences may change throughout the year – can help you to create a more supportive home if you let them inform your purchases and decorating decisions. It can be helpful simply to 'lean in' to the seasons, too. Rather than resenting the cooler winter months, for example, embrace the idea that we are almost different people throughout the year, and embrace the feeling of hunkering down with blankets and candlelight during the darkest nights in contrast to enjoying the feeling of open, billowing curtains and less clutter during the warmer months.

Above: The generous floor-to-ceiling picture windows help bring a generous slice of forest-feels inside. A similar effect could be achieved at a smaller window by adding plants to the floorspace below and hanging a few plants from the ends of a curtain pole, too.

Below left: Everything about this spaces oozes warmth: the predominance of wood, used both across the floor and in much of the furnishings, is complemented with the soft terracotta feature wall framing the living space. A foraged branch makes for an innovative, natural light fitting.

Bottom right: Not having a direct view into nature needn't prevent you from getting biophilic benefits. Studies have shown that simply looking at a depiction of nature - be it a wallpaper print featuring tree motifs or artwork depicting a forest scene - can still evoke a calming effect.

Bringing nature indoors

Several recent studies have shown that spending about 90 per cent of our lives inside (split mainly between home and our place of work) is the norm, so it is more necessary than ever to incorporate the natural world into our interiors. There are, however, a number of ways – involving both sweeping changes and smaller details – we can turn our homes into biophilia-supporting machines.

Water can be overlooked as a mindfulness-enhancing design element, particularly inside the home. So-called 'blue mind science' shows that seeing and even just hearing bodies of water can lower stress levels. An indoor water garden is a compact and beautiful way of inducing watery relaxation, and is easy to set up in any transparent container. Simply put a layer of sand and/or pebbles in the bottom of the vessel, plant it with aquatic plants and fill with fresh water. And, while pet ownership isn't ever to be taken lightly, a fish tank ticks multiple wellness boxes, providing ambient sound, moving water and also the joy that comes from tending another living being.

Opt (where possible) for natural materials that will retain their looks to create a connection to nature: a rattan chair that reveals the variations in its cane, for example, rather than a piece that has been treated to a heavy coating of synthetic gloss colouring. Lookalikes, such as a printed wood-effect laminate rather than solid wood flooring, won't bring quite the same benefits as the real deal, but there's still something to be said for surrounding yourself with sympathetic evocations of natural materials.

You may also wish to consider the five elements of life (fire, air, water, wood and metal) that stem from the Chinese philosophy of *wuxing* and are used heavily in feng shui. Ensure that your home contains a good balance of these elements, such as tactile metals, warmth from fires (or radiators) and candles, grounding natural woods, representations of water (which can include mirrors as well as more literal water features) and objects literally derived from the earth, such as ceramic decorations and stone flooring.

See also page 112: Crafting with nature

Above left: Slim vases like this can offer striking displays of single plants, or go to town creating more of a miniature seascape in a larger container using a mixture of aquatic plants. Alternatively, go small-scale and source a marimo moss ball to keep in a jar, as an 'alternative pet'.

Above right: Collecting dried twigs or branches on walks can make for beautiful, ethereal decoration in the home – just ensure you only remove already fallen branches so as not to affect any wildlife (if in doubt, only take plants or flowers considered as weeds or invasive to that area).

Below: An all-over wood experience can feel immersive and soothing. While different woods are used here, they share a similar warmth, creating a tonal look overall.

The benefits of owning houseplants

The humble houseplant has undergone something of a PR makeover of late, after a couple of decades languishing as a retro throwback. Now it's a ubiquitous addition to any design-savvy home – but for many more reasons than simply good looks.

Plants are a key component of the biophilic home, and numerous studies have revealed a plethora of health and well-being benefits linked to being around, and caring for, plants. The University of Exeter conducted an experiment that revealed how a plant-filled 'green' (over a foliage-free 'lean') workspace increased productivity by 15 per cent as well as lowering physiological stress, increasing attention span and improving well-being. NASA has studied the effect of houseplants in the home, revealing that they can 'purify and rejuvenate air … safeguarding us from any side effects associated with prevalent toxins', and suggesting keeping at least one plant per 30 sq. m (100 sq. ft) to garner these benefits. There's even evidence that simply touching soil or compost that contains 'good' bacteria and organisms can help to regulate our immune systems and lower the risk of inflammatory diseases, which are linked to stress-related disorders.

Flowers (and flowering plants) are also relevant. While filling your home with cut flowers all year round is costly and probably unsustainable (picking your own or buying local, seasonally grown flowers is far better for both the environment and your bank balance), there's much greater benefit to bringing home a few pretty blooms or simple garden cuttings than their appearance. A behavioural research study conducted by Rutgers University revealed that the mere presence of flowers 'triggers happy emotions, heightens feelings of life satisfaction and affects social behaviour in a positive manner far beyond what is normally believed'. A more sustainable trend for dried flowers has emerged in the last few years, and since many last for months or even longer, they can be a great budget-friendly way to bring a guaranteed long-lasting display into the home.

See also page 64: How to create a mindful totem

Above: A large collection of houseplants can offer a striking style statement (along with the aforementioned health benefits). This display shows how, by sticking to an otherwise limited, natural palette – in this instance, decorating predominantly with natural wood and terracotta pots – you can fit a lot into a small space without it feeling overwhelming.

Below left: If you're feeling creative, grab some fresh or dried flower stems and try setting up an 'ikebana' arrangement (a Japanese art form for creating minimalist, sculptural plant or floral displays that directly depict nature). Alternatively, a 'flower frog', like this one, offers a simpler way to get the look.

Below right: Keen horticulturalists show ever more inventive ways to sneak extra greenery into the home, particularly in smaller spaces where surface areas are limited. Wall-mounted and hanging planters offer one space-saving solution, or get creative with styled plant vignettes: something like this could also work on a smaller scale using air plants.

Grow your own kitchen garden

The kitchen can inadvertently become a wasteful place, and, disconcertingly, a third of all food intended for human consumption never makes it to our plates. By growing our own edibles in the kitchen, as well as giving ourselves sustenance, we are reaping the feel-good benefits of surrounding ourselves with natural materials and creating something from scratch, encouraging our brains to slow down and smell the … basil.

If you've ever tried to keep supermarket-bought potted herbs going, you'll probably have come to the conclusion that it simply can't be done. But it's not you, it's them; potted herbs in shops generally look so lush because they contain several smaller plants squashed in together in a way that isn't sustainable for long. Instead, try growing your own from seed. A windowsill is the ideal spot, as long as it's not draughty. Herbs fare best when watered from below, so choose a vessel with drainage holes and its own drip tray (disguise a less-than-lovely plastic container with a fabric wrap, or repurpose a past-its-best ceramic or metal pot by placing some masking tape over the area you intend to drill, then carefully going through it with a masonry drill bit).

You can create your own mini circular economy of sorts by cultivating vegetables from food waste. Collect a few pretty glass jars and dishes to house your cuttings in, then place vegetable ends cut-side up in shallow water and wait for nature to do its thing. Some vegetables, such as spring onions (scallions), can simply remain living in water while you cut off what you need for cooking; others will require potting up and moving outdoors once roots have formed. If surface or windowsill space is limited, think laterally. For anything not too large or heavy, fix magnets to flat-backed containers and attach to your fridge, or screw on to the side of an end cabinet. Alternatively, set up a string of hanging planters in front of a window for sun-loving potted veg. If you're struggling to get anything going, particularly in the dark winter months, an LED grow light could help (adjustable desk-style angled options work well and are generally unobtrusive, or you can fit a grow-light bulb into an ordinary lamp).

Above left: Most herbs would be more than happy in a sunny spot like this, but if you find you're struggling, try cultivating a crop of single-yield micro greens, which are very simple to grow from seed, to garnish salads and sandwiches instead. Or, for something self-replenishing, cut-and-come-again lettuce can fare well in a kitchen.

Above right: Make it easy to save scraps for cultivating while you cook by keeping a collection of small receptacles close to hand for transferring cut ends directly into. Keeping them all contained on a tray makes them easy to move around if you need space.

Below: For a completely foolproof solution, consider investing in a hydroponic grow pot, which allows home horticulture to grow without soil (or indeed much intervention at all), using nutrient-rich, pH-balanced water and lighting systems. Becoming ever more popular in urban areas, there are various aesthetically pleasing designs on the market, from rustic mini greenhouse styles to more minimalist, spaceship-chic looks.

Tip

Save supermarket potted herbs by separating the individual plants (remove from the pot, soak the root ball, then gently break into smaller sections) and repotting in a mix of compost (make sure you use peat-free, which is a far more sustainable alternative to peat) and topsoil. During the warmer months, use an appropriate organic fertiliser every few weeks to top up the soil nutrients. Many are for both indoor and outdoor use, so check the container for the best dilution for houseplants.

Living shapes

Our environments are dominated by straight lines and boxy shapes, but in nature there's no such thing as a right angle, and biologically we have a far closer connection with rounded corners and imperfect edges that mimic nature. Cocooning natural spaces or structures, where we feel protected and sheltered yet not totally disconnected from the outside world, can enhance our feelings of safety, which allows us to relax more easily.

While knocking down your walls to create a fully curved home is hardly practical, it can nonetheless be useful to consider ways of understanding these natural shapes and integrating them into the home, in order to bring a sense of peace. Fractals, the repetitive shapes and structures that occur commonly in nature, might at first glance appear chaotic, but actually they follow a formulaic geometric structure of organic patterns. In the natural world this could be the veins on a leaf or the unique pattern of a snowflake; in design, it's the gentle swirls in a marbled wallpaper or the seemingly random splatters of a poured painting.

Translating this to home design might mean bringing in natural fractals, such as pressed flowers and leaves in a frame or a shelf holding sea urchins or pine cones, or something more interpretive, such as a foliage-inspired abstract mural. Animal print, such as Dalmatian, leopard or zebra, and similar uneven, repetitive patterns can also be thought of as fractal, and can produce similar benefits for the brain. When it comes to the bones of the house itself, a spiral staircase counts as a fractal shape, as do wall tiles patterned with gently textured waves.

The concept can also loosely relate to the idea of harmonious proportions and the 'rule of thirds', both of which often appear in nature and suggest that – to a degree – what we find beautiful is partially innate. In art and photography, many popular compositions adhere to these rules, and in styling, arrangements using odd numbers and varying heights are often advocated, as is the repetition of key shapes within a piece or scheme.

See also page 128: Fashioning harmony in the home

Experiments conducted by the physicist Richard Taylor since the 1990s have revealed that looking at images with a high fractal content increases the brain's production of 'feel-good' alpha brainwaves. This nautilus shell, with its gentle rotating curves, certainly fits the brief.

Plants for purpose

Flowers, plants and herbs have been used for centuries for their purported healing benefits and continue to be used today, whether in traditional form or through essences, capsules and tinctures. Selecting plants for our interiors and our outside spaces based on their particular benefits, rather than just for their specific looks, can be its own form of mindfulness, allowing us to home in on the scent of soothing camomile if we're feeling stressed, or stick our nose into some feisty peppermint for a heady hit when we want to feel invigorated. You could even set up a 'tea garden' of flowers and herbs to boil up in case of illness, incorporating such healing plants as echinacea (said to help protect against colds and flu), mugwort (for menstrual problems) and lemon verbena (for trouble with digestion).

Vertical gardens and moss walls are becoming increasingly appreciated for their sound-insulating properties, as well as the visual softness and connection to nature that they provide. Said to reduce sound by up to 10 decibels (depending on the application), they can also improve overall air quality. Retailers offer ready-to-hang modular systems to set up yourself, or you could construct your own by lining a box frame with plastic (use old carrier bags, rather than new plastic sheeting) and fixing chicken wire to the front to hold everything in place. Fill with soil before adding succulents, moss or any other plants with shallow root systems, such as bromeliads and ivy.

To enhance the mental-health boost that nurturing living things can bring, not to mention the cost savings and much-reduced carbon footprint when compared to buying new, try propagating your own plants. Different plants vary in their preferred methods of propagation, but there are two main strategies to get them started: placing offcut stems from herbaceous plants in small glass bottles of water; and lying fleshy succulent leaves or offsets (small replicas of the parent plant) on a shallow bed of plant-specific potting compost in a waterproof container. You may find it useful to group the bottles or containers on a tray, so that you can move them easily into direct sunlight when you need to clear the space.

Above: Propagating plants could be thought of as an act of wellness in its own right. Taking the time to carefully nurture a new cutting into life requires focus and regular input until it is established, and the experience can be hugely rewarding.

Below left: Making your own foraged teas is both satisfying and decorative, and you needn't necessarily go further than your back garden. Wild daisies are said to help fight inflammation and strengthen the metabolism – simply steep the heads in boiling water for five or ten minutes before straining.

Bottom right: Displaying your cuttings en masse as if they're a floral centrepiece, rather than tucking them away in a corner somewhere, stops your space feeling cluttered with itty-bitty jars and vases. To visually group them further (and to make them easier to move if you need to), try standing them all on a tray.

Tip

Aloe vera is a great plant to have on standby in the kitchen in case of burns. Just break off a leaf and apply it directly to the skin after soaking the burn in water. You can even make your own juice from its leaves – search online for recipes. It can also be a great option for a bedroom as it emits oxygen at night, which can help purify the air and aid breathing.

Visually soften your tech

It's well documented that over-dependence on and addiction to household tech, and smartphones especially, is causing anxiety to soar and having a detrimental effect on our circadian rhythms through too much exposure to blue light. Therefore it stands to reason that trying to help it blend better into our homes, as well as bringing in a few tech-management measures, will bring back some biophilic balance.

The TV is usually one of the most obtrusive items in an interior space, given our predilection to design entire rooms around it almost as if it were a mirrored deity. Trying to lessen its visual impact by housing it away from a focal part of the room, such as in an alcove rather than proudly mounted on a chimney breast, is a good starting point. You can now buy clever TVs that transform into mirrors or artworks at the touch of a button, but for an existing, 'ugly' unit, consider buying or building a cabinet with fold-back or pocket doors, to disguise it completely when not in use. Opt for designs that will hide additional tech, such as cable TV boxes or external speakers, and trailing wires – a vintage cupboard or sideboard could easily be reused for this purpose, and will help the set-up look less otherworldly.

When it comes to other spaces, such as the kitchen, manufacturers of white goods are fortunately beginning to offer more considered designs over simply offering bog-standard white or brash stainless steel appliances (though often, simply hiding said appliances behind built-in cupboard doors or cabinet curtains is your best bet).

The other common cause of visual discomfort in the home is the computer, especially since working from home has become the new normal for so many. If you have to use a repurposed corner as a workspace, consider a bureau cabinet with doors, or simply a large wooden box in which you can hide laptops and files once you're done for the day. Quite apart from the visual impact of the technology itself, accidentally eyeballing an overflowing pile of paperwork during an evening off isn't conducive to rest.

See also page 34: Conduct your own 'greenover'

If you're shopping for new kitchen gadgets, as well as ensuring they have good eco credentials, look for designs with a less 'flashy' feel, such as kettles with wooden (or wood-effect) handles, or toasters in a gently toned, matt powder-coated finish rather than cold, shiny chrome. You might even be able to inject a little fun, as this witty collaboration between designers Poodle & Blonde and Haden exemplifies.

Tip

Smartphone addiction has been linked to depression and social anxiety, so it's wise to watch our usage. Consider creating a phone 'amnesty' during mealtimes or before bed by setting up a storage area complete with chargers and a plug socket, to help get yourself out of any mindless scrolling habits. Customise a storage box by cutting a small hole in it to allow the cables to exit at the back, to keep things tidy yet practical.

How to: create custom plant holders

Procuring (or propagating) plants is only half the story when it comes to plant ownership: they also need appropriate vessels to house them in. Some may be capable of living in the plastic inner pots they were supplied in, though many will need repotting into something larger to encourage growth. Either way, stylish ceramic pots can become costly if required en masse, so a little creativity applied to less visually inspiring containers can be helpful.

Wrapping with cord

You will need:
- Unwaxed natural cord sash
- Superglue
- Natural string or macramé cord
- Scissors
- Sturdy card rectangle

1. At the bottom of your pot, glue down the start of your cord, then continue wrapping it around the pot travelling up, pulling it tight as you go and adding dots of glue along the way to secure it. Stop just shy of the pot's top, leaving enough excess cord to cover the remainder.

2. Make your tassels: take your macramé string and wrap it around the card rectangle (the larger the card and the more wraps, the bigger the tassel, so experiment with size first). Cut through the string at one end of the card then lay down flat: you'll now have a bunch of equal-sized string pieces. Take another piece of string and tie it tight in the centre of the lengths, then fold the string lengths back over themselves. Tie another piece of string near the top of the bunch to give you a tassel shape.

3. Tie your tassels onto the excess cord at the top of the pot, using the string holding that central knot in place, then continue gluing the cord into place before cutting off at the top.

Adding a fringe

You will need:
• Paint (leftover emulsion paint or tester pots, or try acrylic or chalk paint)
• Paintbrush
• Fringing – brush and bullion work well, or make your own using fabric
• Double-sided tape
• Fabric scissors

1. Paint your pot – most paint should adhere easily to terracotta, though plastic may require several coats. Coated ceramic surfaces may not take as well – try priming first, or opt for spray paint instead. Allow to dry.

2. Take your trim and cut to length. If making your own using fabric, lay enough down flat to cover the pot's circumference, then cut evenly upward in strips, stopping around 1 cm (½ in.) from the top. Felt, suede or leather work well as they don't fray.

3. Add a strip of double-sided tape at the top of your fringing, then press in place around the top of the pot. Experiment with different looks, such as a second layer of fringing, or cutting the ends into differing lengths.

Distressed effects

You will need:
• Black paint
• Charcoal
• Ash
• Wood glue
• Paintbrush

1. Paint your pot (the same advice applies here as to the fringe project, but if you want to site this outside, terracotta pots are the most durable).

2. Gather up your charcoal and grind it into a chunky powder: for a small pot you could use charcoal drawing sticks, but for anything large, barbecue briquettes are more economical. There are no hard and fast rules, but you will probably want at least a couple of handfuls per average-sized plant pot.

3. Coat the bottom half of your pot with wood glue then, while it's still wet, scatter the charcoal over it (try laying the charcoal onto a plastic sheet then rolling it over, or just get messy and pat it on with your hands). Add the ashes to the top in sections for a scorched look. Once you're happy with the result, let it dry.

You could also try:

• Roughly wrap a piece of paper around your pot then tie with string for a rustic look (simple brown kraft paper looks great, or opt for pretty giftwrap). Cut away at the bottom to allow for drainage.

• Wrap a birch bark strip (search online for suppliers) around a straight-sided pot, securing with twine.

• Decoupage works well on most pot surfaces. Tear up some patterned paper strips, dip into a watered-down PVA glue solution, then press onto your pot, building up in layers until completely covered.

• Old metal jelly moulds make for cute planters. Line their base with pebbles to prevent roots getting waterlogged.

• Rattan 'belly' baskets disguise ugly pots wonderfully (if said pot has drainage holes, ensure that you place it in a drip tray so it doesn't rot the basket's bottom).

CHAPTER 6

Craft and Creativity

Creativity can refer to many different things: an inventive way of thinking, the process of making something new, or simply an aptitude for turning innovative ideas into reality. But we often have the wrong idea about it, thinking of it as a gift that we either have or don't have, or conflating it with skill, despite the fact that the two are not inextricably linked. Creativity is something we can increase, nurture and improve with practice and patience, given the right conditions, an open mind and the desire to do so.

It's also an important element to bring into any home, and research has shown a number of ways that creativity can enhance mindfulness (and vice versa). Although we often think of it in relation to visual arts-based subjects or activities, it can be applied equally to science, writing and music (among other topics), although the focus of this chapter is on how crafts and creativity can converge to help make our home more mindful and supportive. Bringing both creativity and craft into your home might mean making pieces to display there, or introducing other handmade works of art and craft, and research indicates that both approaches bring benefits for our well-being.

A study at the University of Helsinki in 2013 revealed that certain genes associated with creativity are directly related to brain plasticity (where learning and experience causes cells to modify or even create new connections), as well as fluctuations in serotonin, which can lead to depressive moods when low but evoke feelings of happiness and well-being when high. Read on to find out what mental and visual benefits incorporating creativity in your home might bring you, too.

The well-being benefits of embracing handmade

Various neuroscientific studies have shown that using our hands to create can help us feel empowered and valued, tapping into an almost primal need. The same satisfaction can be felt when we surround ourselves with other makers' works of art and craft, too. Undertaking creative pursuits expressly to improve our mental health dates back more than a century. One of the earliest examples involved soldiers who had survived World War I being prescribed basket-weaving classes in the hope that this simple, repetitive task might help them to recover from their ordeal in the trenches. Craft has even been linked with slowing the onset of dementia, reducing blood pressure and distracting the mind from chronic pain.

Yet grabbing a set of chalk pastels or a pair of knitting needles when we've not engaged in creative making for many years can activate deeply entrenched feelings of fear. By remaining receptive to inspiration and working out ways to reconnect with our innate natural creativity, we can make and consume in a way that's far more rewarding than simply decorating by numbers at a big department store. Bringing more creativity into our lives often just requires a small commitment to switch an unrewarding pastime (such as scrolling on your phone) for something new and fulfilling, and removing as many of the barriers to doing so as possible. Even something as simple as keeping a sketchbook out on the coffee table, and committing to spending ten minutes doodling or colouring in abstract shapes each night in front of the telly, can help to loosen us up and get the creative juices flowing.

Consider, too, how a more fluid, creative approach to your interior could open you up to a more interesting and personal home. While most cohesive schemes have some sort of defining 'red thread', this can be far less literal than matching curtains with carpets. Instead, focus on other relatable elements, such as how a rough-textured ceramic vase could subtly link to the pattern in a favourite artwork, or how redefining the angles of a room by painting them different colours at abstract points could make the space more interesting overall.

Above: A dedicated space to create could be something as simple as a trestle table tucked away in a corner, easy to put away if the space is required for other activities. Having somewhere set up and ready to create in can help remove that first procrastination obstacle.

Bottom left: A recent study by the BBC Arts Great British Creativity Test showed that creativity (whether partaking in it or being surrounded by it) helps block out stress and anxiety, with a quarter of test participants revealing a craft-based pursuit was their favourite stress-busting activity.

Bottom right: Think outside the box (or rectangle) when it comes to the feature wall. Decorating your home can be considered an act of creativity and self-expression, so why not have a little fun and create your own special definitions? Create painted zones using different colours and rounded shapes for a calming effect, or try diagonal or even jagged lines for an energetic atmosphere. Artistic skills aren't necessary, though low-tack masking tape will help.

Tip

Do you want to use social media more productively? Focus on following creative accounts that inspire you (simply mute the rest) and set the intention of sharing your own achievements online - not for likes, but for accountability.

Find your passion

We have a habit, as grown-ups with busy lives, of thinking we need a justifiable reason to take up a creative hobby, other than 'merely' enjoyment and mental well-being. What's the point of dedicating time to learning how to do something non-practical if you're not going to turn it into a side hustle or new business venture – right? Stepping out of the productivity headspace and doing something simply for the sheer pleasure it brings is just as valid – but where should you start if you don't have a natural leaning to one particular medium?

First, think about what tends to lift your spirits, then investigate ways to translate that into a hobby. Do you love gardening, or walking in woodlands or fields? Maybe something related to flowers or foliage would suit you, such as pressing flowers to create artworks or greetings cards, or working with dried blooms to make decorative seasonal wreaths? If you are mathematically minded and prefer numbers and precision over fluid self-expression, woodworking or welding might be more your thing.

Consider your personality type, too. Deciphering whether you're an archetypal 'A' or 'B' type could help you determine the type of activity that will leave you feeling fulfilled. A-types are generally high achievers who are thorough and conscientious and like to follow a plan from start to finish, whereas B-types prefer a more experimental approach to tasks, and value exploration and 'going with the flow' over focusing on the outcome. With a craft such as pottery, an A-type might prefer to quietly develop the wheel-throwing skills to create a matching set of tableware, while a B-type might tend towards experimenting with freestyle hand-building and layering up different glazes, just to see how they come out. You could decide to lean in to your natural inclinations, or use them as a challenge, trying out something that's just outside your comfort zone. Type A might find liberation in trying out abstract painting with an unplanned, free-flowing and even 'messy' approach, while the focus of a far more ordered activity such as cyanotype printing or pinhole photography could encourage a type B to be more structured and orderly.

Above left: Pressing flowers can be a rewarding 'slow' craft, allowing you to preserve your best-loved blooms (or choose the favourite flowers of a loved one to create a personalised gift). If you don't have a flower press, simply use a hardback book, placing baking or parchment paper in between the blooms and pages to absorb any moisture. Stack several books on top, then set aside for a few weeks.

Above right: If you haven't attempted a still life since your schooldays, rather than trying to recreate a Dutch masterpiece on the first sitting, focus on more abstract details – paint a representation of what you see using only coloured circles, or create a 'wet' watercolour, washing water over your paper first then adding the colour once it's still wet, allowing the different paints to run and flow into interesting shapes and combinations.

Below: Patchwork quilting is a very precise and organised craft that relies on complex plotting and problem-solving on graph paper before you even get to the needle-and-thread stage. If you have an engineer's mindset, you may find this suits your sensibilities.

Collect and curate

You needn't get your hands dirty (literally or otherwise) to bring the mindful benefits of handicrafts and art into your home. Slowly building a collection of lovingly handmade objects, rather than buying a job lot of decor in one hit, can bring its own reward. The work of the researcher and art historian Jonathan Fineberg examines the way simply looking at or engaging with visual art can help the development of connections in our brains, providing a workout for the mind rather than the body, which can increase feelings of well-being.

You certainly needn't be an expert to begin a collection, and it doesn't have to be highbrow and costly, so if scoring floral oil paintings by amateur artists at garage sales is your thing, roll with it. Our appreciation of a piece increases if we truly understand it, so don't be afraid to ask questions of the seller or maker; as your interest grows, so will your knowledge and, in turn, your enjoyment. Building a collection needn't be time-sensitive or pressurised, either, and the act of considering items you love (whether eyeing up a purchase or simply something you enjoy looking at) can lift the spirits and will give direction to your overall scheme when you do decide to add new elements.

In home decor terms, collections are invariably at their strongest when grouped, be it art on a wall or an assembly of decorative porcelain pots. Depending on the object, you could opt for a graphic arrangement – setting out seashells starkly in size order – or create something more naturalistic by clustering similar items in a vignette on a shelf or cabinet. Smaller objects could be confined to a wall-mounted printer's tray, using its myriad compartments as miniature display spaces, or even line the top of a deep picture frame. Try following the classic stylist's rule of grouping arrangements in odd numbers and differing yet not too dissimilar heights, to create drama without losing balance. Or group objects by colour, perhaps even creating a spectrum (rainbows are said to symbolise joy and positivity).

See also page 92: Living shapes

Above: Through clever shopping and styling, it's possible to introduce a creative, homely feel to any space (case in point: this sitting area is actually the communal lounge of a B&B). Often, by loosely choosing a theme (or having the theme choose you), everything all magically works together in a way that somehow always misses the mark when we shop solely with our eyes and not with our heart.

Bottom left: Decorating with natural treasures can hold a somewhat primal appeal, syncing our minds with the outside world and with things passed. Dried flowers, as one example, offer a snapshot in time and can be displayed sculpturally or used within more elaborate displays.

Bottom right: Displaying favourite treasures under a glass cloche can give them more gravitas, as well as providing protection for anything fragile. Ledges and mantelpieces offer a handy space to create little styled vignettes that might otherwise get lost on larger surfaces.

Communal crafting

The craft economy has boomed in the last decade, and sales of craft equipment have grown as stressed-out smartphone addicts turn to home crafting and workshop activities to combat loneliness or a perceived lack of purpose. Even politicians have advocated for the 'social prescribing' of arts- and crafts-based communal activities as a way of improving mental health and reducing dependence on antidepressants.

Not only can participating in a communal craft activity be a great way to learn new skills and meet like-minded people, the shared experience can also leave us feeling connected with fellow group members on a psychological level, and is even said to enhance altruism. Local Facebook groups, communal noticeboards or Insta-following creatives based in your area can all be useful ways to find out about local craft events, but if going out to undertake a course or attend an event isn't an option right now, consider setting up your own at home. It needn't be anything grand, just an excuse to gather like-minded friends to craft, chat and learn a new skill, and also offering (in true communal spirit) an opportunity to share tools.

Whatever you're making, you will most likely need to gather around a communal table. If yours is too small, bring one in from the garden and cover it with a wipeable tablecloth, or try placing a few smaller tables together (placing books under feet to equalise their heights, if necessary), or ask a couple of guests to bring along foldable or trestle tables. Consider any special requirements for your crafts, such as extra power sockets for electrical equipment and task lighting. Don't put too much pressure on yourself to create the perfect setting – that is unhelpful to anyone's well-being – but you may find it rewarding to use such a gathering as an opportunity to have fun styling your space with extra thoughtful, handmade touches. This needn't mean anything fancy; even decanting craft supplies into pretty containers or glass jars counts as practical decor. The point isn't to present something 'perfect', just to provide a good excuse to try something out for a non-judgemental audience.

Above left: If you're setting up a still-life painting class, consider the viewpoints offered by each seat at the table - setting up a number of smaller vessels and objects might afford more variety to participants than one large arrangement.

Above right: The Swedes have a lovely term – as they do for many things – to describe the idea of taking a mindful pause in which to make things, socialise and enjoy a special meal using seasonal produce. Known as a *syjunta*, the practice is now being borrowed by other cultures, too.

Below: If you love an excuse to experiment with a new crafting technique, combine a personal project you've been itching to try out with producing the decor for your crafty gathering. Creating macramé chair backs or making clay charms to go on guests' glasses could offer an outlet that you can then use in your styling.

Tip

Crafting can be a surprising force for good, and many grassroots 'craftivists' or 'guerrilla crafters' attend events or protests using handmade pieces to make political points. Search online for events in your local area, or organisations you can contribute to remotely.

Embracing imperfection

There's something undeniably special about handmade pieces that bear a visible human touch, or proudly display the scars of age; they connect with us in a way that mass-produced pieces simply cannot. Some crafts, such as ceramics, date back thousands of years and are deeply entrenched in our psyche. Potters often describe the deeply meditative state they enter when creating their work, as breath, body and mind are forced to tune in completely to the act of creation. The slight imperfection of a wobbly rim or a thumbprint in the glaze (deliberate or otherwise) helps us to feel connected to the piece and, in turn, its maker. Even simple details, such as a mug with a handle that bears the subtle dent of its maker's thumb, offer shapes that are far more ergonomically pleasing for our own hands to hold.

An emerging trend in the West is the ancient Japanese art of *kintsugi*, which is as much an ethos as a specific technique. Translated as 'golden joinery', it is the art of repairing broken ceramics using a gold alloy, chosen to embrace the changing nature of the object and enhance its beauty rather than simply disguising the damage (although today *kintsugi* kits are available to buy, using glue rather than gold). *Kintsugi* pieces encourage us to accept suffering and damage as part of our journey. Treating your own broken bits in this way – either to repair them or to combine them with others to create something completely new – can be rewarding in itself.

This ties in with the concept of *wabi-sabi*, another Japanese philosophy celebrating impermanence, imperfection and incompleteness. Patchwork is one example, where scrap materials are used to create something greater than the sum of its parts, and it is especially effective if they hold personal meaning, such as remnants of clothing once worn by a loved one. Some techniques, such as *boro* stitching, follow a similar philosophy and can be a great repair option if you lack fine sewing skills but are keen to get creative and reuse something worn. The technique turns *sashiko* running stitches into part of the design, to visibly mend as well as customise.

Above: Quilts are possibly one of the best examples of an 'embracing imperfection' craft, often made using remnants and scraps to create something far greater than the sum of its parts. They can also be a clever way to allow sentimental items, such as old baby clothes that are no longer needed, to live on in a different guise.

Below: When pottery breaks, it's never even and always unpredictable. By honouring these scars in gold, it can help us remember that we have the power to take something deeply damaged and, rather than 'fix' it, find a way to allow it to continue to be beautiful and useful within its new altered condition.

Tip

Try *kintsugi* for yourself by mixing a two-part epoxy-resin glue suitable for ceramics to create a paste, before sprinkling in a little fine gold 'mica' powder and applying to the broken edges of pottery. Hold in place until firmly fixed together.

Crafting with nature

We have already discussed the benefits of being surrounded with nature, but what about using foraged natural materials in crafts, for a double hit of crafty eco well-being goodness? Foraging is practically part of our DNA, and can strengthen our ancient connection with nature. However, it's wise to observe the etiquette: stay in public areas; take only what's abundant there; don't dig anything up; and, on the beach, be aware that removing shells can damage natural ecosystems, so leave the bucket at home.

You may find there's plenty in your back garden to appreciate, starting with charming leaves and flower heads to press and frame, or use in other craft projects. Reconsider favourite childhood crafts, such as tree-bark rubbing or collecting leaves and twigs as alternative mark-making tools for painting, all of which can produce surprisingly sophisticated pieces if you use more sympathetic colours than the brash paints and crayons of yore. Nature also provides great stamps for decorating paper, cards and even gift wrap. Keep things simple by coating pressed leaves with acrylic paint, then pressing them down carefully on to paper to form an abstract pattern or a deliberate design such as a mandala. You could also try more advanced leaf-printing techniques such as steam or hammer printing (search for tutorials online), or revisit the humble potato for use as a stamp, carving out shapes with a scalpel to create repeat patterns on paper or fabric.

When it comes to wood, opting for reclaimed or 'green' woods is a great way to reuse otherwise waste material for craft or DIY. Scrap wood such as old floorboards and fence posts, or even the ubiquitous wooden delivery pallet, can be turned into something new (Pinterest is awash with ideas for what to do with these pallets, from planters to full-on pieces of furniture, depending on your skill and willingness). Look out for 'sustainable' woods, too, which are felled by forest stewards as part of landscape management, making them a natural by-product.

See also page 84: The importance of biophilia

Above: Design collective MR Studio London use a mixture of pressed flowers and delicate lino cuts to create a sustainable range of art prints. Using a refined palette and loose, foraged style reflects the natural materials they grow and work with.

Below left: Another heritage craft enjoying a resurgence in popularity is wood carving, with city dwellers such as Grain & Knot opting to connect with nature by hand carving spoons, bowls and art objects. Many professional turners and carvers now offer workshops and online kits for keen hobbyists to try. For a fully pre-industrial-revolution experience, seek out classes or makers who use an old-fashioned shave horse or pole lathe, which requires no electricity or petrol to operate.

Below right: Designer Vanessa Arbuthnott chose the humble potato print, often thought of as child's play, to create an organic geometric striped pattern for her Artist's Collection range, endeavouring to retain its texture once the final design was sent to production. If it's good enough for the professionals …!

Go with the flow

If you're looking to try craft as a way of harnessing the effects of mindfulness, a 'flow' activity is a great start, and there are plenty of options that you can do at home without requiring much in the way of specialist kit or artistic skill. According to the originator of the term, the psychologist Mihaly Csikszentmihalyi, a 'flow state' is one 'in which people are so involved in an activity that nothing else seems to matter; the experience is so enjoyable [that they] will continue to do it even at great cost, for the sheer sake of doing it'. Reaching flow state requires working on a task that demands complete concentration, where actions and awareness merge and time seems either to slow down or to speed up, yet the task suits our ability level and we feel in control (and experience a sense of reward when we finish it).

Most crafts can bring about a flow state, although an activity involving repetitive actions should, according to Csikszentmihalyi, bring 'a perfect immersive state of balance between skill and challenge' to be most effective. Undertaking such activities can trigger beta waves in the brain, which are shown to fire up when we're engaged in problem-solving, and can bring soothing feelings when we focus fully on a flow activity. Just remember to keep things realistic, or you might end up overwhelmed and put yourself off.

Wool-based crafts such as knitting, weaving and crochet, along with sewing projects such as needlepoint and appliqué, can be worked on very easily from the comfort of the sofa, but if you prefer something that gets you out of the house, ceramics, woodworking and life drawing are all good options, particularly if they entail a social aspect. The trend for adult colouring books as a mindful pursuit, which swiftly became a worldwide phenomenon in 2015, tapped perfectly into the framework of what makes a flow state, offering a creative pursuit with a modicum of personalisation (the user can choose which colours to use), yet removing the prospect of 'blank page' procrastination, which might feel terrifying to those who haven't done anything artistic since childhood.

Above left: Keeping your craft supplies close to hand can be a good way to help nip any procrastination in the bud. A set of easily accessible knitting needles and wool in chic wire containers and charming ceramic pots will make it easy for you to dive in and clear away easily.

Above right: Embroidery is a great option if you're looking for a flow craft that's easy to pick up and put down (or work on in front of the TV). If your drawing skills aren't up to much, look for kits online with pre-printed patterns.

Below: Artist Laxmi Hussain's life drawings share close ties with free-flowing organic, natural forms, and are testament to the beauty you can create by letting your hand instinctively move across the page.

How to: have a go at new arty pursuits

If you're keen now to try out some creative crafting but are still not sure where to start, try easy process-driven, intuition-led exercises to get your creative juices going and build your confidence. The aim should be to concentrate on enjoying the process rather than worrying about the result, so put any judgement aside and enjoy getting those hands dirty. Here are three different subject areas to try, with minimal skill requirements and an equally minimal starting outlay.

1. Play with paint

Paint splattering Unleash your inner Jackson Pollock: gather some tins of leftover household emulsion paint or buy some inexpensive poster paint and set up a large sheet of paper on a table (surrounded by protective sheeting – things are going to get messy). Experiment with flicking and splattering the paint across the paper, seeing what effects different brushes give, allowing the paints to dry and layering them up.

Dripping Lean a canvas or thin piece of wood against a protected upright surface and pour paint of different colours carefully down it from the top. Acrylics work well, or use leftover household emulsion, watering the paint down before transferring it to a jug or empty sauce bottle for use. Stick to straight-down drips, or experiment with moving the canvas mid-flow to produce different effects.

Feathering Paint your paper or canvas all over with a single colour, then leave to dry. Paint a second colour over the top, roughly following a straight line (horizontal, vertical or diagonal), and let that dry, too. Then add tiny amounts of the two colours to two brushes, and work in messy, irregular strokes over the point where the two colours meet, so that the colours seem to blend into each other in an ombre effect.

Put it into practice Try scaling up these techniques by using them on furniture, a door or even a feature wall.

2. Create a collage

Pop art Attempt your own interpretation of classic 1950s Pop art by cutting out images that speak to you and using them to make an abstract re-creation of an everyday setting, such as a living room, park view or street scene. The aim isn't necessarily to represent anything, just to consider what might make an interesting composition.

Matisse cut-outs Create abstract shapes by tearing up different-coloured pieces of paper and layering them up to create an interesting pattern inspired by a view or artwork you like.

Colour gradation study Take small swatches of different-coloured paper (or even natural elements, such as slices of fruit and vegetables or a collection of fallen leaves), and arrange them in a spectrum design, allowing the different colours to flow into each other in an orderly or freehand manner. This will teach the eye to home in on subtle differences between colours.

Put it into practice You can also use collage to decorate a flat-fronted object such as a wooden storage

box. Stick the paper pieces down with PVA glue then add a few coats of watered-down glue over the entire composition, leaving it to dry between layers, to keep everything stuck down and create a wipeable surface.

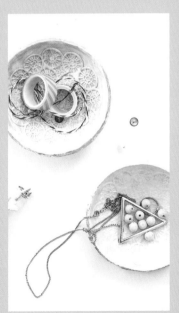

3. Work with clay

Note: We suggest using air-drying clay, which is not only affordable and easy to use at home without specialist equipment, but also usually eco-friendly. Follow the manufacturer's instructions regarding how long to leave the clay to dry.

Imprint dishes Use a textured object such as a doily, leaf or craft stamp to decorate the surface of a piece of rolled-out clay, experimenting with making repeated marks. If you're not happy with the look of anything, simply squish it up and carry on playing.

Pinch pot Roll out a piece of clay thinly and shape it over a bowl, glass or other container. Pinch together the excess clay before cutting off the folds, then smooth using a wet finger.

Remove from the support vessel and smooth the inside of your clay piece in the same way.

Marbling Add a few drops of acrylic paint or food colouring to pre-kneaded white (or light-coloured) clay, then roughly mix, stopping before the colours are fully blended.

Put it into practice Use rolled-out clay to create small trinket dishes or larger plates, gently turning up the edges to create a slight lip. Leave it flat and cut it out to form coasters or hanging pieces for a wind chime. Pinch pots can be used to house dry goods or simply as decorative pieces; if you want to use yours as a plant pot or vase, ensure you use an inner container, since the clay won't be waterproof. Marbled clay can look chic rolled into balls to make beads (pierce with a skewer before the clay dries).

CHAPTER 7

Edited and Organised

Many of our homes today are fuller than ever before: the average American home, for example, contains a whopping 300,000 'things', yet being surrounded by a surfeit of clutter is known to raise cortisol and keep it elevated throughout the day, increasing the risk of chronic stress. The 80/20 principle is often applied to Western homes, whereby we use 20 per cent of our possessions 80 per cent of the time (and vice versa). The psychology professor Joseph Ferrari describes clutter as 'an overabundance of possessions that collectively create chaotic and disordered living spaces', which can in turn create a stressful home environment, particularly if you're a sensitive soul who feels (metaphorically) weighed down by disorganisation.

This chapter aims to demystify why it can be so hard to have a good clear-out, as well as offering a plethora of design and organisational ideas to help. The solution is not necessarily living with less, but living better and surrounding ourselves with objects that support, rather than hinder, our lives and our well-being.

Keeping it fresh

Our brains have evolved to prefer order over clutter, predictability over chaos. Yet unchanging views or routines can lead to hedonic adaptation, whereby things remain consistent and we simply get used to them and fail to notice – or derive any novelty or pleasure from – them. Whether we bring in a new addition to a room or totally rethink its design, that new must-have cushion or transformative sofa reconfiguration quickly becomes – literally – part of the furniture. Seeking out ways to reverse this effect can bring excitement into our homes and lives, and reignite our appreciation of everyday objects.

Of course, that's not to suggest you should be redecorating every few months, but by being savvy we can reduce this hedonic adaptation without necessarily spending any money. For starters, consider 'shopping your home': reviewing your possessions afresh and considering ways you could switch things up a bit, either by moving small accessories from room to room or reconfiguring the layout of a given space. You might find that pulling together disparate artworks from several rooms to create one impactful feature wall in your living room will feel new and exciting, or you might decide to paint a kitchen dresser a completely different colour and move it into the bedroom to house favourite shoes and handbags. Perhaps there are other small-scale ways you could redecorate, such as painting a drab door in a vibrant hue, to bring in a burst of positive colour as you enter the room.

If you're keen to bring in new furniture or accessories but don't want to commit or are short of funds, there are other options besides buying. The residential and luxury hire market has boomed in recent years, particularly in the fashion industry; more and more companies loan designer handbags and frocks, and grassroots 'swishing' groups encourage like-minded women to swap designer outfits. The interiors market is slowly but surely following suit, and there are now companies that offer hire of both vintage and designer furniture and art.

Picture ledges are a brilliant hedonic-adaptation management device, allowing you to easily switch around artworks, ornaments or book and magazine covers to create an entirely new look without needing to touch any DIY equipment or spend any money. Painting them the same colour as your walls allows them to blend into the background for a fuss-free look.

Meaningful minimalism

There is a common misconception that living minimally simply means having a home that's devoid of colour, pattern and ornamentation as well as 'stuff'. A truly successful minimalist home may well be lacking in detritus (not to be confused with possessions), yet it contains an undeniable warmth achieved through the most beautiful (although not necessarily the most expensive) natural materials and carefully handcrafted accessories. Decorative elements are included purposefully, and only if they bring character and soul. The decorative and functional are both viewed with the same discerning eye, while emphasis is placed equally on everything from the tiniest detail – light switches and cutlery – to the big-ticket pieces and overall spatial design, allowing the eye to roam unfettered by anything that might distract it.

The prospect of a truly minimal home is beguiling, particularly for those of us who feel burdened by our belongings or overwhelmed by visual stimulation. But it is foolhardy to assume that simply eradicating all pattern and disposing of most of our worldly goods under the guise of 'minimalism' will truly make us happy. There will be some people who find that this allows them to be their best selves, but for others, living so sparsely will bring unanticipated downsides. At our core, we all need to feel safe, comfortable and protected, and a completely ornamentation-free space with no cosy fripperies might leave some feeling exposed and vulnerable.

You can incorporate key elements of minimalism into a somewhat fuller home, however. Consider undertaking an audit of all that you possess and applying the well-known William Morris adage to it – if it's not useful or beautiful (bonus points if it's both), it's probably time to move it on, sell or donate it. For anything that qualifies purely as ornamentation, is it displayed to best advantage or simply mucking in with the rest of the clutter? And for anything essential yet not display-worthy, such as toilet rolls or tins of paint we intend to (definitely) use, would rethinking storage improve the organisation and flow of the space?

See also page 14: The importance of slow living

Above: If you have a large bedroom, installing a false wall like this can offer a great opportunity to keep your clothes (and clutter) tucked out of sight, leaving you a clear view of, well, clear space (or some aesthetically chosen pieces) instead. Room-divider screens can also be a great way of concealing any less-than-lovely corners or hiding dual-use aspects of the room, such as a home office space lurking in a corner.

Below left: We often imagine airy modernist apartments when we think of minimalist design, yet the same principles apply in any space. A characterful building, such as this one, provides a charming canvas and the pared-back, minimal interior styling allows its period details to shine through.

Below right: Large picture windows are on many people's aspirational wishlists, yet they can leave inhabitants feeling exposed if there's nothing to dress them (particularly in urban environments, where there are increased privacy issues). Opting for a less fussy treatment, such as shutters or simple curtains that blend in with the surrounding walls, helps create privacy without compromising the clean lines of this style of glazing.

Seamlessly integrated storage

We tend to fill the space we have, regardless of how much stuff we actually need. So, before buying or building extra storage (or if you're factoring it in as part of a larger home renovation), take the time to go through your possessions to gain a clear picture of what you need to keep and, of that, what you'd like to display or hide away. Also, notice any existing storage that is simply too difficult to access or maintain (a tell-tale sign is piles of stuff waiting to be put away on or near it, because accessing it is such a chore). Could this space be configured better? Sometimes we get so used to something that we accept it as it is, even if we could do something about it and despite the fact that it might be bugging us daily (that hedonic adaptation effect again).

Built-in storage usually offers the most bang for your buck, particularly in awkward areas, such as sloping roof spaces or extra-high ceilings in rooms with limited square footage, where off-the-peg solutions may not fit. Consider whether your preference is for streamlined spaces or a more organic (yet charming) hotchpotch of items out on show. If minimal is your thing, you may find that investing in something substantial – an entire wall of handle-less, built-in floor-to-ceiling cupboards, say – will enable you to store any necessary yet unsightly items well away while ensuring they're easy to access when required, allowing you to keep the open elements of your space clutter-free. If floor space is limited, consider sliding or pocket-door systems and add castors to the feet of any bulky furniture that might need to be moved out of the way for access. In smaller spaces, it is a good idea to ensure that objects both serve their intended function and provide bonus storage; try using an ottoman or old chest in place of a coffee table, and choose standard storage furniture for big-ticket purchases such as beds and sofas.

Above left: Thanks to its handle-less design, you'd barely register that this bedhead is actually surrounded by storage cupboards. Incorporating shelving space above the bed eliminates the need for bedside tables. Although this shelf niches inwards, the idea could be reversed in a small space by buying (or building) a storage headboard, providing space for a glass of water, lamp and a book.

Above right: Mixing both hidden and concealed storage can give the best of both worlds, incorporating display space alongside private spots for items you'd rather keep out of sight.

Below: Leave no space to waste; if you're incorporating built-in seating into a room, it's always worth trying to double this up as storage. Opt for lift-up seat sections, or go with handle-less storage doors underneath instead of simply boxing it in. Push-to-open mechanisms allow for a totally seamless look, or go for a discreet finger pull or strip.

Creating a stress-busting #shelfie

Being unable to find everyday items ranks highly as a household and family stressor, so including functioning storage solutions – whether hidden or on show – is an admirable goal for sanity. Storage where the objects remain visible can soften a space that might otherwise feel stark and unwelcoming, as well as (in theory) making it easy to access your daily essentials. The aesthetically minded, however, risk getting sucked into styling the perfect 'shelfie' (those oh-so-expertly curated shelves that are showcased on social media) and inadvertently creating an area that looks great yet ends up getting trashed every time you want to find anything, or consigning genuine everyday foodstuffs to the far-flung corners of inaccessible drawers in favour of displaying a dust-laden cake stand that you never use.

To avoid this, you need a modicum of common sense and some decent storage containers. In the kitchen and bathroom particularly, decanting is both pretty and practical: it can physiologically 'turn down' visual stimuli and lower feelings of overwhelm by reducing the branding in the home and eliminating the often garish, attention-grabbing tones of commercial packaging. Shelves lined with rows of glass jars or stackable containers full of foodstuffs or everyday toiletry supplies allow you to see at a glance what you've got and how much is left, making it easier to keep on top of the shopping as well as creating a calming, homely vibe. Supplement a stock of official Kilner, Weck and Mason jars by reusing glass food jars to keep costs down, and keep shorter containers and everyday ingredients nearest the front.

Shelf dividers can also help you to organise your space, particularly if there's a generous gap between shelves. Of course, your shelves needn't be shelves at all: an old wooden drinks crate, complete with internal compartments from its days as a bottle-holder, could be hung on a wall to house smaller items, from ties to toys; or sneak in raised storage on a countertop by gluing feet to the bottom of a wooden offcut to create a small raised ledge.

See also page 22: Turn down your home

Above: Keeping kids toys accessible might be more practical than tucked away, but this needn't mean compromising on looks. By utilising small wicker storage baskets on open shelves and leaving nicer-looking toys on show, this display isn't just style over substance. Think creatively when it comes to containers – old cake tins would also work well here for collating smaller collections of toy cars or building bricks.

Below left: Give a disparate collection of glass jars a more unified look by part-painting them all with glass paint, or add some colour using sticky-backed plastic. If you're storing everyday items, look online for ready-to-buy designs that incorporate relevant written labels, too.

Bottom right: Clutter can cause irritability and even spike anxiety levels. Shaker-style peg rails can help make this an easy battle to conquer – in a kitchen or dining space they can be useful for smaller items like scissors and shopping bags, while in a bedroom they can help alleviate any 'floor-drobe' issues.

Fashioning harmony in the home

The ancient Chinese art of feng shui – in a nutshell, the practice of using positive energy (*qi*) to bring harmony to our environment – may seem mystical and far-fetched, but it is worth taking the time to understand its principles and how they can relate to the modern, mindful home. The practice encompasses everything from the overall architecture of the home to the objects in it, following the idea that calm and its converse, chaos, both inside and outside the home, are inextricably linked and can influence each other. On a fundamental level, this makes sense: the mind, body and environment all affect one another, and a chaotic space overflowing with clutter can leave us feeling as though we're living inside one long to-do list. The same is also true of a space so tightly controlled that a single object even slightly out of place sends its owner into a mental tailspin.

In practical terms, creating positive *qi* in a space comes down to removing any physical barriers we may have inadvertently created, such as piles of clutter blocking access to cupboards, or a room configured so that we walk directly into obstacles such as sofa backs or sharp corners, which can feel unwelcoming and possibly even unnerving to both guests and residents. Clearing out items that are said to contain negative or draining energy, such as dead plants and broken homewares (unless we're willing and able to resurrect or repurpose them), will also help to reduce clutter and therefore, it is to be hoped, stress.

Feng shui often advocates placing furniture in a 'commanding position', referring to the optimal spot for key pieces such as beds and seating. It dictates that the entrance of the room should ideally be visible from this spot, without the piece being placed directly in front of it. This makes sense physiologically, since our fight-or-flight response is programmed to react to potential danger, and so sitting or sleeping facing directly out of a doorway – or, conversely, having no view out of the room at all – could make us feel vulnerable. If you can't accommodate this into the layout of your home, consider placing a piece of furniture or even a tall plant to break direct sightlines, or adding a freestanding mirror to give you that missing view.

Everything in its place: feng shui warns against overlooked corners, which can collect clutter (and store stagnant energy). Incorporating simple storage, like this ledge, helps eliminate these issues while making best use of the space. There's also some design sense at work here: in the bedroom, feng shui practitioners recommend using curvy lamps and bedside tables to harness supportive and romantic energies, while design-wise, balancing out the rectangular blockiness of a bed with rounded accessories either side can help the space feel welcoming rather than austere.

Visual tricks to create order

Our brain is constantly bombarded with far more data than we can process, so it's forced to filter and concentrate on what it thinks is important – but it determines this based on what we consciously focus on most, which is often negative thoughts or distracting behaviour, rather than what we actually *want*. If we employ methods that allow us to process key information visually as well as verbally, the brain finds it easier to tune in, enabling us to break down large tasks into actionable chunks and visualise how we might achieve them (and, as a result, making them more likely to happen).

Mind maps and kanban boards, which work in a similar way to visualisation boards (see page 56), are two ways of achieving this. The kanban board consists of several columns, generally starting with 'to do', leading to 'in progress' and finally 'done', and each task is written on moveable cards to keep everything flowing from left to right. Mind mapping – a visual form of note-taking similar to the spider diagram – gives the opportunity for creative brainstorming; a central issue is written in the middle and we work outwards from there via sub-categories. Incorporating sketches or even images with your notes can help your brain process and recall the information quicker than words alone.

Brain 'tagging' can also help certain tasks flow with greater ease. We all have triggers in the home, be it navigating through piles of last night's dishes when you're trying to make breakfast, or constantly struggling to find keys and appointment slips when you're rushing out of the door. To help form habits, such as automatically taking five minutes to tidy the kitchen before bed or hanging up the keys as soon as you come in, elect a particular object or activity as your cue to act, and stick with it. For example, every evening, use the switching on of the kettle to trigger that final tidy, or the act of taking off your jacket as a key-hanging trigger. If you fight through the procrastination, it'll soon become muscle memory and you'll find yourself automatically doing it before you've registered what you're up to.

Above left: When it comes to mind mapping, design yours in a way that resonates with you. You might prefer the flexibility of sticky notes so you can move ideas around, or opt for different coloured pens to denote different tasks or idea flows. Post-its in fun colours and shapes could help sneak a bit of joy in, too.

Above right: If you're having to hot-desk on the dining table rather than at a dedicated home working station, try arranging your work corner so there's some sense of separation from the rest of the tabletop (especially if other family members might also be using it for eating or doing homework at the same time). A pen pot, lamp, notebook and a few accessories could make all the difference to visually divide that section.

Below: Work from home? Try setting aside five minutes at the end of each day to partake in a little knolling – the technique of arranging your desk space in a pleasingly geometric way – after you've clocked off. It'll doubtless lift your spirits when you sit back down the next day (and makes for a great Instagram flatlay, to boot).

Tip

While physically writing down ideas can help them form more clearly in the mind, if want to ensure you have access to your notes across all your devices or when out and about, try going virtual. Organisational apps like Trello and Asana allow you to create online kanban-style boards for many different topics, while more in-depth CRM systems like Dubsado and Notion are like a virtual assistant (and brain-dump). Create mind maps online using programs such as Ayoa and Miro.

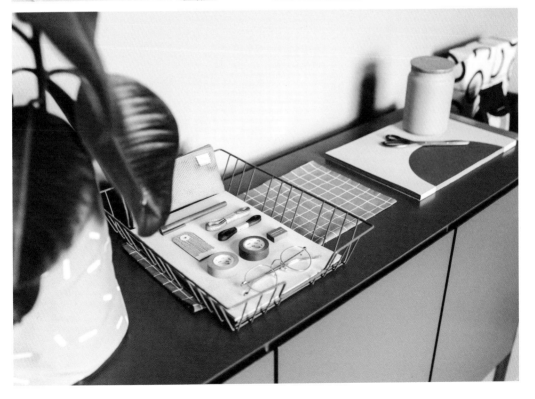

Meaningful decluttering

Decluttering is often unavoidably linked to emotion, whether that be the struggle of letting specific belongings go or the feelings driving the reasons we might be over-accumulating in the first place. For many of us, it is simply a case of the so-called endowment effect, the idea that we perceive our possessions to be of more value than they actually are, which makes us hesitant to part with them even if we no longer want or need them. Research from Yale University shows that, in extreme cases of hoarding disorders, throwing out certain belongings can cause a reaction in parts of the brain identical to those involved in feelings of sadness and even physical pain.

To ease emotionally charged decluttering, consider ways of honouring the items you're parting with. It may sound silly, but it's not a bad idea to spend a few moments mindfully thinking about the pleasure owning each object has brought, and of the person or memories it brings to mind. Photos of things that make us feel happy but that we don't need to keep (such as every single 'artwork' your child has ever created) will bring back the memories and raise mood-boosting serotonin when viewed in the future. Or give Grandma's unwanted tea set to a good cause (after all, studies have shown that giving rather than receiving really does make us happier). If in doubt, ask yourself whether you'd pay for this item if it were in the shops right now.

There may come a time when you feel you need help with decluttering. If you're finding things genuinely difficult, perhaps asking a friend or engaging a professional who can gently guide you through it all with a caring yet impersonal touch could be the boost you need (as well as the emotional support, having someone else physically handle difficult items, rather than you touching them yourself, can help you emotionally detach from them). Throughout the process, it might help to keep in mind the vision of living in a clutter-free yet supportive space, feeling happy, free and balanced.

Above: If you've undertaken a big clearout and aren't sure what best to do with some of the leftovers, look out for any type-specific charity initiatives in your area for items a charity shop might be unable to take, such as toiletries for women's refuges, tents for rough sleepers, old yet functioning cameras and electronic equipment for adult educational and training charities, or bicycles for refugees.

Below left: Japanese decluttering expert Marie Kondo is well known for asking us to assess what within our homes 'sparks joy' and suggests surrendering anything that doesn't, though what works best for many is finding a middle ground. If seeing certain items is weighing you down yet you have nowhere to conceal them, consider 'upgrading' certain pieces once they are nearing the end of their useful life, slowly replacing them with items that have a resonance or an aesthetic you find pleasing, over the purely perfunctory.

Below right: Having a designated space for favourite ornamental toys and paintings in a child's bedroom or playspace can help stop clutter spiralling. It also allows toys that are no longer played with yet hold sentimental value (such as hand-me-downs from grandparents) to live on as decor, keeping the toybox free for everyday favourites.

133

How to: make a wellness-boosting wall chart

If we're not careful, mindful living can feel less like treating ourselves to some much-needed self-care and more like another entry on the never-ending to-do list of life. Trying to fit everything in can even become a competitive challenge, where we berate ourselves if we miss a morning meditation or forget to make our tea in an appreciative, mindful way and instead knock it back with a biscuit while scrolling through social media. It can even trigger feelings of guilt if we do indulge, prompting us to mull over the myriad things we should be doing instead, or question whether we're even worthy of a relaxing half-hour off with a good book (ahem, Netflix).

Visual prompts, particularly charts or tracking aids, are eminently useful for reminding us what we want to do, achieve or turn into automatic habits. Rather than creating a rigid 'to do' system with possibly unachievable goals listed each day, however, use such prompts to flag up the wellness activities you'd like to incorporate into your life, then mark down what you actually do and when, to build up a picture of your days, weeks and months. You might be surprised to discover that you're doing far more than you thought.

Don't forget, though, that the goal isn't simply to go through the motions of ticking things off, but to be present throughout and to look objectively (and with grace) at *why* you're not fulfilling some of the tasks you would like to. This can help you to determine whether you've simply been busy, are aiming too high right now, or are avoiding sitting down to document your emotions because you're struggling with something and are anxious about having to confront it. Or maybe you're putting the needs of everyone else above your own because you don't think you're as important as your partner/friend/boss? Having a monthly overview can be just as useful as filling in your chart daily, and it'll provide you with that double hit of visual and written stimulation, helping the practice to stick in your head and become a habit.

Consider creating, too, your own minimal requirements ('minimals'), meaning the achievements you feel are wholly realistic and attainable (rather than ambitious aims) for anything you're hoping to form into a habit. The key is to make these easy to achieve, to help set you up for success (so if you find you're not meeting them, reduce them next month then look to work back up – or question if there's an underlying reason). You could then use a highlighter to mark each time you do more than your minimals, giving yourself a visual affirmation of your success.

We've created this chart especially for you – you can download it to print out from joannathornhill.co.uk/books/new-mindful-home, or just use it to inspire your own bespoke design. We advise hanging it (use washi tape or poster hangers) somewhere you can access it easily every day, such as on the side of your wardrobe, by your desk or in a quiet corner of your kitchen. We've given examples of how you might choose to fill it in, and we advise homing in on key activities or areas you'd like to integrate more regularly into your routine, then adding or removing as you go. You can also use it to keep a tab on things such as your dominant emotions and even to log your menstrual cycle, to help build a clearer picture of how external (and internal) factors influence your days.

The finished look of the chart is for you to annotate in whichever way resonates most. If you're artistic, you may prefer to create simple sketches to represent each activity on your grid, or you might opt to keep things simple and just assign a different coloured dot or sticker to each entry. If you'd like more space to write, consider customising an oversized monthly wall calendar and copying everything onto that instead. If you'd rather not have yours out on show, stick it inside your wardrobe door or somewhere else you access throughout the day, so you don't forget about it. Add your own freestyle customisations to it too – perhaps a symbol in the top and bottom corners of each day to indicate your overall mood, so you can see how your activity affected this.

Tip

This chart works well as an overview, but you could also use it to dive deep on one particular issue, or help towards a specific goal, such as turning a hobby into a business, or to record a food/mood diary to help recognise any patterns and triggers.

My Wellness Chart

MONTH

1	2	3	4	5	6	7
8	9	10	11	12	13	14
15	16	17	18	19	20	21
22	23	24	25	26	27	28
29	30	31				

THIS MONTH I'D LIKE TO INCORPORATE

MY MINIMALS

As featured in *The New Mindful Home* by Joanna Thornhill
www.joannathornhill.co.uk/books/new-mindful-home

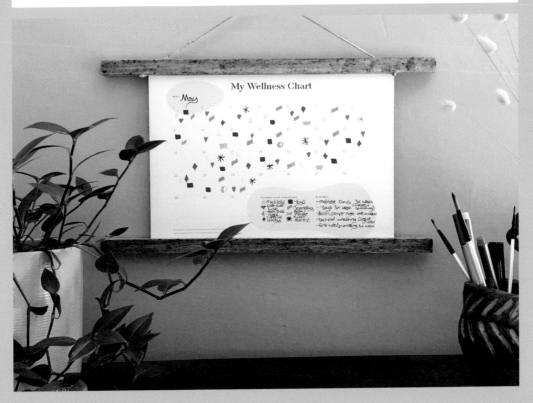

Mindful know-how

USEFUL TERMS FOR THE MINDFUL SHOPPER

Keep these words and phrases in mind when planning or purchasing for your interior spaces.

Anxiety economy Unsurprisingly, as anxiety disorders continue to increase and it is said that around one in three of us suffers, there is a wealth of products aiming to cater for this rising consumer group. All products are not created equal, however, so before panic-buying a half-price 'anti-anxiety' shower gel, check in to ensure you're not simply outsourcing your well-being to an impulse buy that you don't really need or want.

Circular economy Designed to disrupt the traditional 'linear economy', in which we create and consume products made from raw materials, then discard them (or their packaging) once they are no longer required. A circular economy aims to ensure the system feeds back into itself, creating a closed loop. Products are designed to use recycled materials, and constructed with easy repair in mind, then reused or recycled when they reach the end of their lives.

Climate positive Also referred to as 'carbon negative'. A product or an entire company can be climate positive, so look out for this term when shopping. The production of climate-positive products actually *removes* carbon dioxide from the atmosphere, rather than not producing any, giving climate-positive purchases a sustainability gold star.

Upcycling Although many of us are now familiar with this term, it is often used misleadingly. Its original definition referred to the process of using an item that was no longer fit for purpose (a broken chair, say), which might have ended up in landfill, to create something of elevated value (such as a bespoke bench combining elements from several broken chairs). Bear this in mind if you're buying upcycled pieces in order to lower your carbon footprint; a new high-street sideboard that someone has painted with a natty design might not be as green as you think.

Value tagging Championed by the neuroscientist Dr Tara Swart (see page 56), this is a subconscious system by which the brain assigns importance to the information we expose it to, and through which it can give undue weight to a particular object (for better or worse). This can be applied to trends, too; you notice an ombré cushion cover in a magazine and then on a friend's sofa, and suddenly you see them everywhere. Check in with yourself when making design decisions. Do you truly desire whatever it is – or is your brain telling you what it thinks you want without checking in with you cognitively?

HASHTAGS TO FOLLOW

Scope out some of these growing tags on Instagram, for a wide variety of #inspo.

#blackpoundday

Founded as a solutions-based approach to supporting the UK Black economy, this hashtag (and its website, www.blackpoundday.uk) acts as a portal for discovering Black-owned enterprise and helping to redress the balance of disproportionate poverty among Black, Asian and other minority communities by supporting their businesses.

#dolessharm

Set up by the journalist and writer Kate Watson-Smyth, this hashtag features shares among the interiors community of products, makes and room decor schemes that aim to have a less harmful impact on the planet through sustainable shopping, crafting and creative reuse.

#knitflixandchill

A cheeky bit of wordplay used to share knitting and crochet patterns and projects, this alludes to the rewarding 'flow state' (the blissful point at which you become mindfully immersed in a creative pursuit) that can be achieved through these gentle, repetitive making activities.

#slowsustainablehome

With a mix of interiors, lifestyle and wellness, this hashtag offers a plethora of ideas to help you harness a slow lifestyle.

ETHICAL ORGANISATIONS

Keep an eye out when shopping to see if the retailer you're purchasing from has signed up to any of these schemes.

1% for the Planet www.onepercentfortheplanet.org
Business members displaying this pledge have committed to giving 1 per cent of gross sales each year to approved not-for-profit partners focusing on environmental causes.

B Corporation www.bcorporation.uk
A global movement aiming to redefine business success, B Corps status is offered only to select companies that are seen as disruptors and changemakers in their industry. Members must adhere to rigorous environmental and societal standards, balancing purpose with profit and using their business as a force for good.

Care & Fair www.care-fair.org
A member-funded organisation helping to improve the lives of carpet and rug knotters in countries such as India and Pakistan, ensuring fair wages and good living conditions for weavers and fighting illegal child labour in the industry.

Declare declare.living-future.org
Focusing on the materials market, a Declare label details where a product comes from, what it's made of and what happens to it at the end of its life. It helps manufacturers, designers and customers to see at a glance if toxic chemicals have gone into an item's production, and that materials such as wood have been sourced sustainably.

Rainforest Alliance www.rainforest-alliance.org
This organisation's distinctive symbol – a frog, symbolising a healthy ecosystem – acts as a seal of approval and is awarded to products that meet the relevant forestry and agricultural preservation objectives.

Resources

A selection of brands, buys and generally clever people to help you build on the ideas discussed in each chapter.

CREATING A SANCTUARY

Shida Preserved Flowers www.shida.florist
An innovative subscription brand specialising in preserved real blooms as a long-lasting, sustainable alternative to imported cut flowers. Arrangements can be shipped in pre-made bouquets or as letterbox-friendly loose stems.

Philips Hue www.philips-hue.com
Offers bulbs that can be dimmed, colour changed or operated remotely via an app, to enable you to adjust lighting to your needs and help regulate your circadian rhythm, without altering any wiring.

Object www.objectstyle.co.uk
A Manchester-based lifestyle store, curating artisanal homewares and directional design objects for an eclectic interior (see their living space on page 17, bottom).

The Every Space www.theeveryspace.com
A sustainable gift and plant shop operating as a residency for other small businesses local to it in northeast London, such as Head & Hands, which offers curated products for self-care and slow living.

Reste www.reste.co.uk
Stocking wares for 'considered living' online and in a beautiful bricks-and-mortar store in Hastings, southern England, Reste's offerings span well-being, utility, beauty and home.

ReChic www.rechic.co.uk
With an innovative USP, ReChic is committed to selling only furniture and home accessories created from innovative recycled materials, including Fairtrade blankets made from recycled plastic bottles, and wooden tables constructed from old shipping pallets.

Native & Co. www.nativeandco.com
A pared-back showcase of the best of Japanese design, featuring household items sourced from specialist workshops and individual craftsmen across Japan.

Instagram accounts to follow:
@curatedisplay Dedicated to showcasing the stylist/photographer Tiffany Grant-Riley's take on Nordic interiors and stylish slow living.
@spicerandwood The popular feed by this store of the same name shares shots of its pleasingly rounded, comforting-looking homewares: think jewel-coloured glazes and cosy cushions.
@karen_haller_colour Karen Haller is an applied colour psychologist, so you can trust her feed to offer psychological insight alongside pretty pictures.

CONSIDERED LIVING

Fine Cell Work www.finecellwork.co.uk
A charitable organisation focusing predominantly on needlepoint cushions created by inmates of British prisons. The charity's aim is to boost the prisoners' self-worth and self-discipline while teaching them an unexpected new skill.

Ian Snow www.iansnow.com
With a history of scouring India for its most interesting artisans and vintage sellers, this family business offers 'maker profiles' for each item, detailing the workers' rights and conditions and clearly stating the eco credentials.

The Colour Flooring Company www.colourflooring.co.uk
Stocks a selection of natural cork, rubber and Okofloor (a green material made from organic castor and rapeseed oils). These vibrant, playful colourways show that eco needn't always mean serious.

Cadeera www.cadeera.com
This new platform for sustainable and attainable designs from a marketplace of hand-picked sellers is a one-stop shop for high-quality yet affordable vintage and new handmade pieces. It also allows the buyer to discover more about styling and design.

Abigail Brown www.abigail-brown.co.uk
Fancy some fauxidermy? The artist and maker Abigail Brown specialises in creating striking, authentic handstitched fabric birds, as an ethical alternative to traditional taxidermy, alongside more surreal, charming papier-mâché animal sculptures.

Kathryn Davey www.kathryndavey.com
If our introduction to natural dyeing on page 47 (featuring Kathryn's work) has whetted your appetite, check out her website to learn more about this fascinating process via her blog, ebooks and online courses.

Original Organics www.originalorganics.co.uk
A smaller-scale alternative to home composting that can work for paved yards and balconies as well as small gardens. Add some bokashi bran to a special bucket, throw in your household food waste and once it's fermented you'll have both compost and liquid plant food.

Instagram accounts to follow:
@oggetto_home Dreamy, pared-back spaces imbued with this interiors brand's ethos of authentic, tactile furniture and accessories for a thoughtful home.
@theoldpotatostore Who wouldn't love to rifle through a stylist's prop kit? Karen Barlow sells a range of uniquely worn and gently faded vintage accessories from her own prop cupboard supplies exclusively via her grid pages (see her styling on pages 6, 30 and 87, top right).
@ridge_and_furrow The interior designer Elle Kemp's converted Victorian pigsty is period (im)perfection at its very best (as featured on page 35, bottom left).

MINDFUL OBJECTS

Margo in Margate
www.etsy.com/uk/shop/margomcdaidart
Margo McDaid's bobbed female characters –
emboldened with slogans such as 'be brave' and 'be
yourself' (see page 51, top) – remain wildly popular for
their simple graphics and empowering messages.

Coppermoon www.coppermoonboutique.com
Coppermoon offers a range of small shelving pieces
designed for displaying crystals (see the 'teepee' design
on page 55, bottom left), but its spiritually based designs
– featuring motifs such as triangles and crescent moons
– would also work wonderfully for displaying other small
trinkets and treasures.

Mela www.melacomfort.co.uk
Weighted or 'calming' blankets – studded with glass quartz
pellets, designed to weigh you down gently to foster a
sense of calm and alleviate tension – are said to help ease
muscle tension and reduce stress hormones. Mela offers
a 'try before you buy' option to ensure it works for you.

The Crystal Healer www.thecrystalhealer.co.uk
Headed by Philip Permutt – a crystal expert regarded as a
leading authority in the field – this site holds a staggering
array of crystals suitable for all requirements and budgets.

Yoga Clicks www.yogaclicks.com
A charming selection of home yoga equipment and
natural complementary items such as eye pillows and
wheat bags – great for exercise and meditation alike.

Buchlyvie Pottery
www.etsy.com/uk/shop/buchlyviepottery
Including ceramic wind chimes representing the different
phases of the lunar cycle (see page 63, top left), this
handmade, slip-cast porcelain range of home accessories
has a charming, natural quality.

Positive Postcard Club
www.positive-postcard-club.myshopify.com
Created by the illustrator and mental-health advocate
Ella Masters as a way of sharing positivity during the
Covid-19 lockdown, these beautifully illustrated, uplifting
postcards can be ordered online for Ella to post directly
to the recipient with your own message.

Instagram accounts to follow:
@energymuse Dedicated to demystifying the crystal
world through informative, educational posts, plus free
workshops to follow via IGTV.
@yogamattershq Inspirational site both for yoga ideas
and encouragement, and for ogling the beautiful range
of ikat print yoga/meditation floor cushions and bolsters.
@contentbeauty An industry leader for eco-friendly
brands, this lifestyle and wellness store shares behind-
the-scenes and inspirational content alongside a vast
selection of well-being wares for home, body and mind.

CLEAN LIVING

Old Fashioned Milk Paint
www.oldfashionedmilkpaint.co.uk
Similar to its chalk counterparts, milk paint is a very
durable product that can give a new lease of life to
furniture made from natural or manmade materials,
such as melamine. Made from basic natural ingredients
(including milk casein, hence the name), it comes
as a powder, ready to mix with water at home, making
it a strong eco option.

Graphenstone
www.graphenstone-ecopaints.store
The brainchild of a chemical engineer, this
groundbreaking range of lime paints is created using
graphene – a type of carbon – through a completely
environmentally friendly production cycle. It's even
climate positive: as the paint dries, it captures carbon
dioxide, purifying the surrounding air.

Pure Thoughts www.purethoughts.co.uk
This (appropriately) thoughtfully designed website
allows you to shop according to your mindful
requirements, rather than simply by product type.
Opt to 'find pause to …' de-stress, focus or reconnect
through a curated range of meditative candles, beauty
products and ritual kits.

Iggy Box www.iggybox.co.uk
A novel way to discover and support small-batch local
candlemakers, Iggy Box offers a subscription service so
that you (or a lucky recipient) can discover a different
ethical brand each month.

Sacred Elephant
www.sacredelephantincense.com
Synthetically fragranced incense can irritate the nose
and lungs, so for the greatest holistic benefit, opt for
sticks handcrafted from only natural resins and oils,
using traditional methods. Sacred Elephant's sticks
are designed to 'enlighten our moods and enliven our
consciousness'; they also smell divine.

The Owl & the Apothecary www.owlapothecary.com
Drawing inspiration from the Dorset countryside, owner
Katy Theakston's self-proclaimed mission is 'to empower
you to create a life you love through positive thought and
mindful action'. As well as handcrafted well-being and
ritual kits, she offers courses and workshops focused on
abundance and gratitude.

Zero Waste Club www.z-w-c.com
Focusing predominantly on kitchen, bathroom and
beauty buys (alongside cleaning equipment such as eco
sponges), Zero Waste Club has a Transparency policy that
means you can see at a glance the average wage of each
artisan or maker who produced your potential purchase –
and even learn their backstory.

Instagram accounts to follow:
@helloglowblog A selection of easy-to-follow tips and recipes for using essential oils and aromatherapy alongside DIY cleaning, decor and craft projects to create a happy, healthy home.
@kindredwild Thoughtful captions with a mindful, Ayurvedic slant to highlight how using Kindred & Wild's handmade small-batch oils and balms can form part of a holistic, mindful lifestyle.
@weezandmerl Innovative makers who recycle waste plastic to form marbled tableware and flat surfaces. Expect mesmerising videos sharing their unique method of 'kneading' and carving the melted plastic to create their wares.

BECOMING BIOPHILIC

Horticus www.horticusliving.com
An ingenious wall-mounted system that allows you to create your own indoor vertical garden, featuring connectable 'pods' that you can configure to your space.

Chalk & Moss www.chalkandmoss.com
With a biophilic focus, this range of homewares, furniture, lighting and home fragrances aims to foster a connection with nature, in order to enhance well-being. There is an informative blog, too.

The Art of Succulents www.theartofsucculents.co.uk
Offering kits for creating your own terrariums and air-plant displays, this site takes the guesswork out of setting up, providing both assembly and care instructions.

Ilex Studio www.ilexstudio.com
Beautiful glass vessels designed to help you grow your own avocado and acorn trees. Balance an avocado stone or acorn in the top chamber and the roots are visible as they form, connecting you to the growing process.

Paper Thin Moon www.paperthinmoon.com
Focusing on natural, seasonal living, owner Claire Holland's beautifully styled shop and blog champion ways to craft and make with nature, such as flower-pressing and foraged wreath-making. She also features a special ceramics collaboration created with her father (see pages 89, bottom left; 105, top left; and 115, top right).

Bloombox Club www.bloomboxclub.com
Created by Katie Cooper, a doctor of psychology, to help spread awareness of the life-changing effects caring for plants can have on our health and well-being. Bloombox offers plant subscription packages to build your collection slowly, as well as a shop for ad hoc purchases.

HumbleWorks www.humbleworks.co
Minimise the garish plastic that's often associated with desk spaces by choosing computer risers and stands made from humble birch plywood – perfect for home hot-desking on the kitchen counter or dining table.

Instagram accounts to follow:
@oliverheathdesign Championing the concept of biophilic design to create positive living and working spaces, Oliver Heath's Insta is a great place to learn more about the movement and see the work of his architectural interior-design practice in action.
@tribeandus Account owner Kate shares ways to combine several children and lots of plants in a small space, for a maximalist yet surprisingly fuss-free look (see for yourself on pages 15, bottom; and 89, top).
@urbanjungleblog An inspirational curated feed born out of bloggers Igor Josifovic and Judith de Graaff's mutual love of plant-filled homes. Follow their feed to join in with plant-based prompts and challenges.

CRAFT AND CREATIVITY

de Winton Paper Co. www.dewintonpaperco.com
A talented watercolour artist and stationery designer, Harriet de Winton branched out into teaching her techniques online in 2020, and runs a popular YouTube channel sharing follow-along painting projects.

Skillshare www.skillshare.com
A veritable smorgasbord of online classes and courses covering myriad craft topics, all taught and filmed by the creators and makers themselves. Many classes are free to watch, although the paid membership model opens up more options and allows you to participate in workshops and group discussions, too.

Craftivist Collective www.craftivist-collective.com
Set up to follow a 'gentle protest' approach to craftivism (the act of using crafted objects to highlight political or environmental injustice), the Collective sells kits to help you make items to add to this growing movement.

Margate Girl www.margategirl.com
Conceived by the furniture and textile designer Zoe Murphy with the idea of empowering 'non-crafters' through monthly letterbox-friendly craft kits (available individually or as a subscription). Each kit contains all you need to create a specific project, be it sewing, drawing or collage, and gains you access to live craft-alongs on Facebook.

Abby Monroe www.abbymonroe.co.uk
A mixed-media artist championing slow, 'quiet' creativity, Abby Monroe offers free downloads and follow-along classes on her site and Instagram feed, focused on developing your own creative practices for well-being, such as art journaling and flower-pressing.

Jolt www.thisisjolt.co.uk
A collective selling handcrafted items, from ceramics and cushions to carved wooden accessories and organic bathroom products, created by people suffering from mental-health challenges. 100 per cent of sales revenue goes to the social initiative www.designsinmind.co.uk.

Humade www.humade.nl
The innovative brand that first brought the Kintsugi home repair kit to the market also offers iron-on golden patches and wall stickers designed to celebrate imperfection creatively throughout the home and on textiles.

Instagram accounts to follow:
@captainsrest The photographer Sarah Andrews, owner of the Captains Rest waterfront retreat in Tasmania, showcases the space's unique decor, featuring artfully styled foraged finds alongside prints of her popular oil paintings (see pages 35, bottom right; and 107, top).
@createaholic Dive into the inspirational boho world of macramé doyenne Fanny Zedenius, whose account shares the myriad ways she uses this craft technique in her home, alongside links to her supplies shop and DIY projects (as featured on page 85, bottom left).
@mary_maddocks Expect examples of this textile artist and content creator's weaving work and DIY projects, which she credits with helping her to stay 'calm and sane'.

EDITED AND ORGANISED

Tylko www.tylko.com
With its fully customisable shelving made to your specified size via a clever augmented-reality app, Tylko sells sustainably sourced wooden storage that is as close as you'll get to bespoke built-in furniture without getting a carpenter round.

Rise Art www.riseart.com/about/rentals
Scared of commitment or like to stay light on your toes? Consider renting art over buying; Rise Art allows you to try out different styles and get a fresh new look every month (great for stopping hedonic adaptation setting in). They will even send you a handy guide to choosing your art and styling it in your home.

Buy Me Once uk.buymeonce.com
Happy to invest in decent, well-made items that should (literally) last you your whole life? Billing itself as 'a movement rather than a shop', Buy Me Once puts every product on its site through rigorous testing, championing the benefits of long-lasting goods over cheap alternatives.

Harth www.harth.space
A disruptor of the traditional rental market, Harth offers various clever ways to rent designer, luxe vintage and otherwise lovely interiors pieces for those who are unwilling or unable to commit to buying bulky furniture.

The Green Gables www.thegreengables.co.uk
An eco-friendly stationery brand that includes gratitude and reflection journals, which are said to harness the positive power of anticipation and reflection to increase your happiness (and they'll look pretty on your desk, too).

Present & Correct www.presentandcorrect.com
A cult stationery brand offering 'office sundries for the modern workspace', with a design-led range of desktop paraphernalia that includes all manner of stylish, chic and useful designs, featuring both cutting-edge brands and unique vintage finds. Perfect for any home study space or homework corner.

Mapology Guides www.mapologyguides.com
A series of innovative illustrated self-help maps that are designed to act as an emotional toolkit as you navigate your journey through life. Suitable for pinning to your wall as a poster or simply referring to whenever you need a little guidance, they cover topics such as gratitude, uncertainty and how to say 'no'.

Instagram accounts to follow:
@jessicarosewilliams Living proof that minimal living can be anything but stark – as evidenced in this eighteenth-century country cottage that is light in clutter yet heaving with character (as seen on pages 23, top; and 69, top).
@hanbullivant Showcasing how a rented home needn't be a soulless space, Hannah Bullivant mixes simple, savvy styling ideas with advice on decluttering to improve both your space and your well-being (her vision boards feature on page 57).
@ingredientsldn The Insta account from the store of the same name heavily features the stunning pared-back Edinburgh home of its founder Nina Plummer, and is the embodiment of her message to share soulful homewares for slower living.

Index

Credits

6 Si Thompson Photography www.sithompson.com/Kirsty Saxon – stylist www.kirstysaxon.com/Karen Barlow – art direction and styling @karen_barlow 8 Dulux-Colour-Futures-Colour-of-the-Year-2020, Dulux UK 10 GUBI 13 borastapeter.com 15 (above) Georgia Burns; (below) Kate Chilver/Instagram @tribeandus/Website www.tribeandus.com 17 (above) living4media/Holly Marder; (below) Kathryn Taylor Photography 19 (above) Dulux UK; (below left) Anki Wijnen, Zilverblauw.nl; (below right) Oak Furnitureland images featured in this book show their 2019 real wood inside and out and sofa ranges. All available at Oakfurnitureland.co.uk; 21 borastapeter.com 23 (above) Jessica Rose Williams @jessicarosewilliams (below left) Kelly Day – This is my home style – @thisismyhomestyle; (below right) Si Thompson Photography www.sithompson.com/Kirsty Saxon - stylist www.kirstysaxon.com/Karen Barlow - art direction and styling @karen_barlow 25 (above) Colin Poole/Photoword Ltd; (below) Photography: Haarkon/Cabin: Settle, Norfolk/Reclaimed materials all Morways Reclaim 27 (above) Colin Poole/Photoword Ltd; (below) Jon Aaron Green 28 Oak Furnitureland images featured in this book show their 2019 real wood inside and out and sofa ranges. All available at Oakfurnitureland.co.uk 29 (left) Photographer: @dabito/Home belongs to and is designed by Jonathan Lo @happymundane; (middle) Anki Wijnen, Zilverblauw.nl; (right) Annie Sloan 30 Si Thompson Photography www.sithompson.com/Kirsty Saxon - stylist www.kirstysaxon.com/Karen Barlow - art direction and styling @karen_barlow 33 (above) Holly & Co Work/Shop; (below) Anna and Tam www.annaandtam.com/Aerende www.aerende.co.uk 35 (above) Plain English Design www.plainenglishdesign.co.uk; (below left) Interior design and styling by Elle Kemp and Martin Gane of Ridge & Furrow; (below right) Sarah Andrews 37 (above) Chloë Heywood/Eden Hall Norfolk; (below left) © living4media/Wojnar, Radoslaw; (below right) Caroline Rowland www.carolinerowland.co.uk 39 Unsplash, Lasse Moller 41 (above) Dulux UK; (below) living4media/View Pictures 43 © living4media/Scoffoni, Anne-Catherine 44 (above left) GAP Interiors/David Cleveland; (above right) © living4media/Syl Loves (below) © living4media/Möller, Cecilia 46 Nicole Mamnati/Design: Clara Le Grelle 47 (above) Kathryn Davey; (below) Anna Carolyn Meier/Mollie Makes 48 Kasia Fiszer Photography 51 (above) Dee Campling @deecampling; (below right) Kasia Fiszer Photography; (below right) Holly Booth @BuimBimmlli @nimuellrina; (below) Photographer - Kathleen Stalzer Bly/Stylist - Alyssa Leanne Hoppe 55 (above) Maria Bell Photography; (below left) Made and designed by Kate from Coppermoon Boutique; (below right) Loupe Images/James Gardiner 57 (above and below) Hannah Bullivant, Stylist 59 (above) www.malacollective.com/Instagram: @malacollective; (below left) Caroline Rowland www.carolinerowland.co.uk; (below right) Oak Furnitureland images featured in this book show their 2019 real wood inside and out and sofa ranges. All available at Oakfurnitureland.co.uk 61 (above) Cathy Pyle www.cathypyle.com; (below) Unsplash, Deborah Diem 63 (above right) Eilidh Weir/www.etsy.com/shop/buchlyviepottery; (above right) Free printable for gratitude jar by Claudia Smith @claudia.smith.wellbeing; (below) Genevra Jolie, Crystal Singing Bowls UK www.crystal-singing-bowls.co.uk 64 © www.projectnord.com. The poster 'Enso' is designed by Ayse Sirin Budak for Project Nord 65 Tadhana terrarium arrangement by Balay Diwa 66 Photo by Emma Lee for Rowen & Wren, featuring table linens and tableware from its Autumn/Winter collection. Visit www.rowenandwren.co.uk 69 (above) Jessica Rose Williams @jessicarosewilliams; (below left) Niina Steinke-Schimmer; (below right) Holly Becker @decor8 71 (above) Alternative Flooring, 01264 335111 www.alternativeflooring.com. Photo credit: 7am Creative; (below) Styling and photography by Melissa Tonkin @teamtonkin 73 (above) Ritual created by Katy Theakston, founder of The Owl & the Apothecary/Photography by Sophie Carefull; (below left) Melanie Barnes of Geoffrey and Grace @geoffreyandgrace; (below right) Lily Resta for Nomad Society www.nomadsociety.co 75 (above) Clare White, Made By Coopers; (below) Julia Watkins www.simplylivingwell.com/Instagram: @simply.living.well

77 (above) Danielle Trofe Design, LLC; (below left) Large planters by Dust London in their Peppermint and Chamomile tea variations @dustlondon www.dustlondon.com; (below right) Cathy Pyle www.cathypyle.com 79 © living4media/Möller, Cecilia 80 Julia Watkins www.simplylivingwell.com/Instagram: @simply.living.well 81 Wendy Graham/www.moralfibres.co.uk/@moralfibresblog 82 Dorte Januszewski, www.lewesmapstore.co.uk, @lewesmapstore 85 (above) Five Acre Barn fiveacrebarn.co.uk Instagram: @fiveacrebarn; (below left) Home of Fanny Zedenius, also known as Createaholic; (below right) Siobhan McFadden Instagram @home__stead 87 (above left) © living4media/patsy&ulla; (above right) Si Thompson Photography www.sithompson.com/Kirsty Saxon - stylist www.kirstysaxon.com/Karen Barlow - art direction and styling @karen_barlow; (below) Photography: Haarkon/Cabin: Settle, Norfolk/Reclaimed materials all Morways Reclaim 89 (above) Kate Chilver/Instagram @tribeandus/website www.tribeandus.com; (below left) Image courtesy of Paper Thin Moon, www.paperthinmoon.com; (below right) Kasia Fiszer Photography 91 (below left) © living4media/Harnisch, Christel; (above right) Aimee Wimbush Bourque - author and culinary creative; (below) KRYDDA Cultivation unit, by IKEA 93 Ferm Living 95 (above) Cate St Hill; (below left) Unsplash, Ornella Binni; (below right) Laura Jenkins (houseplanthouse) 97 © Haden/Poodle & Blonde 98 Created, styled and photographed by Teri Muncey for The Lovely Drawer 99 (left) Photography: Jemma Watts/Styling: Laura Sawyer; (middle) Thejoyofplants.co.uk Styling: Klim productions/Photography: Eric van Lokven; (above right) Photography by Kathleen Beyer; (below right) © living4media/Raider, Peter 100 Marij Hessel, My Attic 103 (above) Kristin Perers/kristinperers.com; (below left) © www.aliceinscandiland.com (below right) Hannah Otto @theottohouse 105 (above left) Image courtesy of Paper Thin Moon, www.paperthinmoon.com; (above right) The desk of Michelle Evans, Creative Director, Roxwell Press. www.roxwellpress.co.uk; (below) Kayleigh Excell - Excell Quilt Co. 107 (above) Sarah Andrews; (below left) Georgia Burns; (below right) Kathryn Taylor Photography 109 (above left) Photography by Jen Chillingsworth – Botanical watercolour illustration by Laura Park of Dear Prudence Studio www.dearprudencestudio.com; (above right) Charlie Goodge www.charliegoodge.com; (below) Unsplash, Annie Spratt 111 (above) Jennifer Causey; (below) Nom Living - Nomliving.com/Photographer: Dele Noga 113 (above) MR Studio London; (below left) Sophie Sellu - Grain and Knot; (below right) Potato cut by Vanessa Arbuthnott to create her design: Hand Printed Stripe. www.vanessaarbuthnott.co.uk/Showroom: 12 Ashcroft Road, Cirencester, GL7 1QX 115 (above left) Carolyn Carter Photography @carolyn_carter; (above right) Image courtesy of Paper Thin Moon, www.paperthinmoon.com; (below) Artist Laxmi Hussain @ thislakshmi 116 Brittany Ambridge/Domino 117 (above) www.juliehamiltoncreative.com - Instagram: @juliehamiltoncreative; (below) Created, styled and photographed by Teri Muncey for The Lovely Drawer 118 Kasia Fiszer Photography 121 @bloggaibagis 123 (above) Hypnos Cotton Origins 8 mattress features sustainably sourced cotton and 100% British wool traceable to Red Tractor Assured Farms. Prices start from £2,859 for a king-size bed set (mattress, divan and headboard). www.hypnosbeds.com; (below left) Studio Gabrielle/Louise Parker/Interior Design & Styling Agency www.studiogabrielle.co.uk Beth Davis/Photographer beth-davis.co.uk @_beth_davis; (below right) Unsplash, Taylor Simpson 125 (above left) Architects and photographs: Heju Studio - www.heju.fr; (above right) Kym Grimshaw; (below) Jon Aaron Green 127 (above) Hannah Otto @theottohouse; (below left) © living4media/Hessel, Marij; (below right) © living4media/Möller, Cecilia 129 @bloggaibagis 131 (above left) Marianne Taylor mariannetaylor.co.uk; (above right) Jemma Watts; (below) Kathryn Taylor Photography 133 (above) Caroline Rowland www.carolinerowland.co.uk; (below left) Architects and photographs: Heju Studio - www.heju.fr; (below right) Caroline Rowland - www.carolinerowland.co.uk 135 Joanna Thornhill

Author's acknowledgements

Writing this book, after quietly researching the topic for several years, has been quite the journey of discovery as I've uncovered the myriad ways our homes are inextricably linked to our well-being. It is something I practise rather than preach, and an endlessly fascinating topic that I have enjoyed delving deeper into every day since first having the idea for this book.

So perhaps I should start by giving thanks for my own humble home: my sanctuary and safe space, which afforded me the ability to explore many of the themes discussed in these pages long before I really understood the mindful benefits of doing so. Since my home has stood for more than 120 years, I think of myself as her current custodian, and after decades of renting I do not take for granted how lucky I am to have planted roots.

A home is, of course, nothing without the people in it. I must give heartfelt thanks and love to my partner, Paul, for his unwavering faith in me and for ensuring I was kept well fed and watered while deep in writing and editing mode, and also to our beloved rescue dog, Stella, whose gentle nudge of the nose lets me know when it's time to take a break from the 'tippy-tappy machine'.

Thanks to the team of amazing creatives who have helped this project come together: to Liz Faber and Zara Larcombe for having faith in the concept, and to Gaynor Sermon for steering it through to this finished product (especially given the curveball of a global pandemic thrown into the mix halfway through). To Caroline Rowland, for her amazingly thorough picture-research skills to find the images that now grace these pages, and to Masumi Briozzo for creating such a stylish layout. Thanks also to all the photographers, stylists, bloggers, designers and brands who have been kind enough to share their images, enabling me to illustrate my points so much more eloquently than I ever could have done with words alone.

Thanks to my friends and family for their unwavering support of my work, and to the various coaching and mentor figures to whom I've been able to turn for virtual and IRL support over the last couple of years. Women supporting women is a wonderful thing. Finally, thanks to my readers and followers for joining me – it's a privilege to have you along for the journey. I hope this book helps to satisfy the soul, as well as the eyes and the mind.

ABOUT THE AUTHOR

Joanna Thornhill is an acclaimed interiors stylist, writer, consultant and trends expert. To discover more about her work and read her posts on the topics of well-being and authenticity in interiors, learn more about her online styling services and tutorials, as well as download a printable version of the wellness chart on page 135, visit her website, www.joannathornhill.co.uk, or follow her on Instagram @joannathornhillstylist. Use the hashtag #thenewmindfulhome to share your thoughts and discoveries about this book with other readers.